Identity Crisis

One family's experience of manic-depression

M. K. Dalglish & Sally E. Dalglish

New Generation Publishing

Acknowledgements

Thanks to Dr Srinivassan, Dr Jim Cox, Dr Morrissey, Dr Choudray, Dr Nair, Dr Imo, Dr Muller, Leslie Jamson and Val Atkins, without whom I would be a victim, not a survivor.

Sally E. Dalglish

To Carol Dalglish, with love

Contents

Chapter 1

Broken Gate

Alex ran out of the house, shouting wildly. He threw himself into his old car and raced off down the twisty track. His mother, taken by surprise, saw him pass the window. She could not catch him now. Then she remembered the gate at the bottom of the lane: it was falling apart and patched up with string. It would take him a minute to open it.

She took her car in pursuit, checking as she went that he had not skidded offside into the beck below. She reached the gateway: no sign of Alex, the car or the gate either. He had simply taken it with him. There were bits of it scattered along the lane. This was no time for collecting firewood. She hoped to catch him up before the lane came out onto the main road, but no such luck.

It was likely that he would have turned left, heading for his brother, Simon, who farmed a couple of miles down the road. And that is where she found him...or rather, she found a dazed-looking Simon and saw beyond him Alex's old car, looking even older. No sign of Alex.

"Have you seen him?" Mum asked.

"What, Alex? Yes, he's just been here. He left his car in the yard there, said he'd crashed it. What's it all about? He seemed in an awful tizzy."

"Where is he now?"

"He went tearing off across those fields."

"He'll get back on the road. I must catch him. I can't stop now. 'Bye."

The drive to the farm hair-pinned off the road: Alex would not take long to reach it. Mum reversed her car, hoping to be waiting for him as he came out onto the road. But he was walking along smartly when she overtook him.

"Want a lift?"

"No thanks." He glowered at her.

Obviously, force was not an option. Suddenly she realised that they were not far short of that popular pub, The Moorcock Inn. He would go in there for sure. Then there would be a panic. She did not linger to persuade him but put her foot down hard and got there before him.

The Moorcock Inn was filled with that happy Saturday atmosphere of a leisurely crowd who haven't a care in the world until next Monday. Mum felt as if she were throwing a hand grenade.

"Could you please call a doctor and the police," she said breathlessly.

No one took any notice of her, though some looked puzzled, as if wondering whether she was mad. The members of staff were too busy serving a full house. She asked for the manager but before he could respond she thought of Alex's imminent arrival and went to the door. He was coming in. His walk had done him good and he agreed to go with her. They got into the car together. She heaved a sigh of relief: not far to go home. Perhaps the crisis was over.

It was not over. The road was twisty and they were travelling at about thirty miles an hour when Alex started to get out. The traffic was mostly going their way. She couldn't stop him so she drew up and let him walk in front of her, heading an ever-lengthening queue. At last the road straightened and cars began to pass. All were commendably patient. A Good Samaritan passed her and drew up in front of Alex intending perhaps to offer him a lift.

This was too much! Panic struck Mum. If Alex got into that car she had no hold over him. Heaven knew where he would go. She gesticulated wildly and blew her horn in agitation. Whether aware or not the Samaritan got out of his car and started talking to Alex by the roadside. They seemed to be quite amicable and in no hurry to move on.

At that moment Simon drove up with a friend. Mum hastily explained about The Moorcock and asked Simon to chase up the messages.

"Where shall I tell them to come?" Simon asked.

"Heaven knows! But I'll try to get him home. Otherwise, your guess is as good as mine."

She left Simon to see what was happening to Alex. He was ready to come home with her now, having enjoyed a friendly chat. Thankfully, she turned off the main road heading with him for home. But as they approached the shattered gate a memory stirred and he didn't want to go in. Mum kept on going past the gate, wondering if her message had got through; whether they would meet the police and what she should do if they did. It might take a bit of explaining.

"I want to see Jim," Alex said as they approached Jim's house.

Jim was an unusual and likable man who lived in a world of his own to whom Alex was attracted as a moth to a flame, especially when vulnerable, as now. Mum was apprehensive but gratefully accepted the cuppa which they drank in the front room, overlooking the road.

A police van went by. Mum wanted to yell, but politely drank her tea. No point in making a fuss. It returned, lost. Mum realised that they had not recognised her car. (Perhaps she was not on the 'wanted' list?) She must try and catch up with them. What then? Play it by ear.

"Well," she said hastily, "we must be going now. Alex, are you ready? Thank you so much for the tea."

Fortunately, Alex was much restored after his little social outing and was ready to go home. Simon drove up and, having adjusted plans, she and Alex went home without further ado while Simon went in search of the police. Alex felt tired and agreed to rest on his bed. The police came and waited for the doctor who would have to make the arrangements with the hospital and would, in any case, have to sedate Alex who was not likely to go willingly.

Mum hated the thought of his going. She would have done anything, anything at all to prevent it. But at the time they knew of no way. As long as she lived, she would never, ever forget the occasion when he had been forcibly removed by the constabulary. She had had to stand there and watch him go, unable to respond to his cries, knowing that she had betrayed him. She and Simon had wept. Simon too was vulnerable.

"To think that a man can be carried out of his own house!" The shame of it was unbearable.

Was it happening all over again now? It had taken such a long time to rebuild the trust between them: the faith that was so essential if he were ever to recover. No good moping. Mum put the kettle on. Nothing like a cup of tea to relieve the waiting!

Sounds of an approaching vehicle raised their hopes of the doctor's coming; but it was another police van: from the city. The first had been locals. They waited. They drank more tea. They talked desultorily – what was there to say? An hour went by, and still no doctor. Mum rang The Moorcock Inn.

"Yes, he was here some time ago. He's not here now."

They waited a little longer before the Inspector made up his mind, "I'm going to call another doctor."

Meanwhile, mercifully, Alex had been drowsing in his room. Mum went up to be with him. His head ached but, as usual, he refused to take any pills. She knelt beside his bed, her arm round his shoulder, gently stroking his hair.

"You're ill, my dear," she said. "You know I can't look after you any longer without help. I'm afraid it means hospital. I'm so sorry. I did try."

How much of this he took in she didn't know. But perhaps the real message was in her arms, her voice and at her fingertips, that she loved him. That he seemed to understand and it was enough. She remembered when her first boy, Charles, was laid to sleep in his cot in the evening and she and Peter had slipped out to walk round the farm and come back to find the baby yelling. Dash it!

Could she never get out with Peter? Evidently, she could not sneak out, so one evening she explained to this six-month old cherub that Daddy and Mummy were going for a walk, that they were coming back and that he would be quite safe. He believed her and slept. There must be something, she thought, in the minds of all of us, whatever age or circumstance that understands a lot more than we realise.

The doctor came at last and was for ordering an ambulance. Mum, aghast at the thought of another hour's wait said, "What's wrong with the Black Maria?"

This was very properly thought to be unsuitable. Mum wished she had listened when she and Alex had difficulty in staying on the narrow seat in that very basic form of transport. Alex was unexpectedly sick. They set off in forlorn procession: two Black Marias. Why two? Mum wondered, not realising that the city van would deliver Al to hospital and return to base but she needed to be taken home, so the local one came along too. It was not until later that she realised that during the hours of waiting the police had been long overdue for relief with not a murmur of complaint.

Chapter 2

New Carpets

How had this come to pass? It was a long story – not all sad. Alex had been a sturdy little boy, full of enterprise and mischief, well able to hold his own with his big brothers and a good friend to me, his sister. His fearless attitude to life endeared him to his grandfather, who was normally rather frightening to little boys. His school reports were full of promise; he narrowly missed a place in choir school and was offered a vacancy in another. He had everything to look forward to. Then came our parents' divorce, not in those days, a foreseeable event.

The bottom dropped out of his world. Perhaps, because he had been so completely safe beforehand, the shock was greater and he found himself defenceless. Like a caddis fly he built his own crust of security and became unrecognisable. He dared go nowhere alone.

"He's all right," they all told Mum. "What are you worrying about?"

She knew but she too was stricken and could do nothing. I was two years his senior, and appeared to keep all their strength up. Alex, Charles, the eldest and I would now live with Mum while Simon, the prospective farmer of the family stayed with his father. I was happy in either household and found new friends at school with whom to have fun and giggle. That at least was good, Mum thought: I was apt to be too serious.

Alas, my newfound frivolity was not all good and had sinister undertones. I had acquired a creditable crop of O-levels and was embarking on the sixth form when the balloon went up. One morning Mum received a telephone call summoning her to the school where I lay, sedated. I had been acting very strangely: wandering at night and talking nonsense. Finally, the doctor had been called and he made arrangements for me to be admitted to the psychiatric wing of Mum's alma mater, St. Thomas's in London.

The full horror of the occasion was masked by the need for action. Travelling to Calne, it dawned on Mum that the sword of Damocles had been hanging over their heads ever since Peter's sister had suffered a hypomanic breakdown when expecting a baby. More had been revealed: she had broken down previously when thwarted in love. And of course there was great Aunt D who suffered from depressions, and Aunt Mary. Their sister, Susan, at the age of twenty-seven, had stood, arms outstretched on a railway track in a bid to stop the first train. It looked black indeed, but Mum had been assured that there was no proof that this was a family matter. If what she had learned at school about Mendel's theories were true, the trouble should have been bred out by now. Peter's sister was the only one of her generation to be affected, and Mum's family had no history of mental ill health.

Now Mum and I were driving along on a beautiful day, me, happy as a lark, talking away nineteen to the dozen, hardly stopping to draw breath. The secretary who accompanied us, alert in the back, noted the dash of foam round my mouth. My diatribe was so rapid that neither woman could keep up with me or understand what I was saying. It appeared to be utter gibberish, but Mum noticed that the flow changed direction whenever I came to a double-meaning word. For instance: tear – tier, bear – bare and so on, like a computer slip, not difficult to spot.

What struck Mum with the force of a hammer-gun, was the fact that some of my words (like "tetrahedron") echoed the esoteric teaching which Mum herself had studied – and failed to understand.

"How can Sal," she wondered, "having gone mad know of such things, let alone understand them?"

Mum had never spoken to anyone of these matters. For Mum it meant that far from being hopelessly lost in some inaccessible wilderness, I was a jump ahead, living on some advanced plane. To her this was thrilling!

The sword of Damocles was not so terrifying after all. I was installed in a comfortable room; looked after by angelic nurses; mixed with patients in a similar state of euphoria: I was in heaven.

Sir William Sergeant had various avant-garde methods of treatment. Mary Thornton, who fell in love with a man who brought her parents displeasure, was put in the Narcosis Ward where each patient lay in an induced coma for three months. Mary did eventually marry her sweetheart but the gruesome experience scarred her for life.

High as a kite, I fell in love with everyone I met on the wards and embraced a doctor thinking he was a patient. I saw a pink aura around staff and patients alike. I was verbose and grandiose. Sir William Sergeant gave me a course of electro-convulsive therapy and haloperidol. The ECT was discretely administered after an injection. Electrodes were attached to the temples to administer the convulsive shock. All I could remember on coming round was the headache. Gradually, the memory cells were damaged.

Mum, sponsored by her father, came up from Sussex to visit every day, doing what night nursing shifts she could, but cutting back on the market research. Our outings were finally followed by discharge. I appeared to be normal, was given my pills and sent home.

Nobody realised, Mum least of all, that this was a very vulnerable, crucial stage, which demanded intensive care – not the hospital interpretation of that term: the spirit has crashed and needed re-building. Mum was over-conscious that an adolescent girl wanted to be rid of the apron strings, and she was anxious not to suggest in any way that my life was undermined.

"It's a setback," she mused, "but Sal is bright. There's no reason why she shouldn't pick herself up and start again. The hospital entrusted her with her pills. Who am I to dent her confidence?"

I went to convalesce with Dad, who had had no briefing to speak of. Not bothering with the pills, it wasn't long before I was out of a window in the locked house on a frosty November night. In my nightdress I scampered in the moonlight up to The Moorcock Inn to meet a couple I'd met during the day. They drove me back to the farm and hooted and called up to the bedroom window. The man was carrying me in his arms.

The sash window shot up.

"We've got your daughter!"

"No! You haven't! We're all locked up!"

They delivered me.

My father's mortification was immense. It was the only time in his life he took his belt and lashed me once on the backside.

The Northern Hospital to which I was taken was not as glamorous as St. Thomas's. All ECT patients had to line up in their dressing gowns in a wretched line outside the Treatment room and it was pretty obvious from the big canisters what was going on when we went in. The treatment was definitely painful.

Mum took me back to St. Thomas's but it was no longer party time. The euphoric patients had gone and the present ones were depressed and depressing. It was down to earth with a vengeance.

Home for Christmas: never much fun with the family divided. I was still on medication, or was I? What was to become of me now? I had had a formidable setback. But must I abandon all hope of a career? I'd started on the A-level course. Could I still catch up? Normally, no trouble, but now, it would be hard going. What else could I do? Mum had the idea that I was a born teacher. I had been studying Latin and aiming to do Cambridge entrance.

I went back to school after the holidays. It was about the cruellest thing that could have happened. After all that treatment and all the earlier damage leading to hospitalisation, I could not pick up the threads of anything we were doing in class. This was compounded by the fact that my memory cells were burnt out, although reassurances had been given that they would grow back in time. It was impossible for my innocent classmates to understand. I was quite unable to keep up or explain myself. I detected giggles and laughter and murmurs of, "Looney bin."

The headmistress suggested that I teach in the junior school and re-start my A-levels in the autumn when my memory cells had come back and I'd made a full recovery. Horrified at the thought of my father forking out colossal school fees for an extra year, I quit and returned home within the week.

The question was: "What do we do next?"

It never occurred to Mum to consult the family doctor. We didn't need him very often and, somehow, mental illness didn't seem to her to come within his orbit. Hospital didn't seem a good place for coming out of a depression, however necessary it was in time of manic breakdown.

After a few weeks I began to pick myself up again. I might have lost a year over the A-levels but it was not the end of the world. I could take it easy for a while and begin during the next academic year. Not at Calne or the local school, but Chichester College of Further Education. In the meantime, having O-level and A-level art, why not fill up time at the Art School?

This was all very fine, in theory, but when the time came, I found it impossible to face people again. Remembering my terrible experience at school, how could I expect strangers to be any kinder? Mum made an appointment at the Art School. It was time to start. I refused to get into the car.

"Why don't you come, just for the ride?" Mum coaxed. "I promise you need not go in if you don't want to when we get there. Mr Canning sounds an awfully nice man!"

We had to walk a little way from the car park and found ourselves at the foot of a long flight of steps. Every one of them presented me with a fresh temptation to flee, but we made it, and were greeted at the top by the kindest of men, who was expecting us. He smiled at my unexpected tears as if they were the most normal reaction. I was soon interested in all he had to show me and happily agreed to start work next day. A summer of creativity soon passed.

All went well until the next hurdle loomed: the college. I managed the first few days, signing on for French, English and Sociology, as Latin A-level was not available. But one morning when Mum was preparing to drop me off on her way to a briefing in Portsmouth, I made no move to get out of the car.

"Come on, dear, out you get!"

No response.

"Don't you want to go today?"

"No."

"But darling, I've got to go to this briefing, or I shan't get the job."

"I can't go in."

Really, this was too bad. Mum was going to be late, and it mattered.

"Do you want to come with me?"

"All right."

Oh well, fingers crossed! This job was far too good to lose. We reached Portsmouth, found a car park and passed a school on the way to the appointed place. The ladies were all assembled, one evidently in charge. Mum asked permission for me to attend. There was room at the back. The demonstrator began and was well into his spiel when I became bored. In a loud voice I attempted to interest my neighbour in a totally different subject. Mum dug me in the ribs and froze, trying to disown me. Heads turned and, finding no response from the other side, I desisted.

It was not long before the break. But for Mum, the writing was on the wall. Clearly, she could not hope that I would contain myself for the final hour. When the break came she was ready to make her way to the table, explain the situation and take her leave. This was easier said than done. Every interviewer seemed to want the attention of the chairwoman as soon as the demonstrator gave them a chance. Being at the back of the room, Mum had a long wait.

At last she was able to make her apologies, and receive assurance that the job was still hers. She looked round for me, but I'd vanished. Eating sandwiches? No. In the cloakroom? No. Where on earth? She asked someone.

"Oh yes, she went out."

Out! But where?

I was not in the car. Could I have gone into the school? The door was open, though everyone seemed to have gone to lunch. Mum looked in, and called. No answer. She met the returning schoolmaster who helped her look and took her to the phone to ring the police. The desk officer took details and told her to stay by the car, so that she could be found. So there she sat, pinioned, unable to continue the search, for what seemed an interminable age – probably ten minutes. No policeman came. Had she given him her number? Was he looking in the right car park? What on earth had happened to him? And what had happened to me?

At last! There I was, in the distance, sauntering along, without a care in the world, enjoying the sunshine and pausing to look in shop windows as I passed. The relief was such that it was no good being cross, and anyway I probably didn't know what I was doing. Still no sign of the police as I neared the car.

"Hello," Mum said calmly. "Where have you been?"

"Oh, I found a carpet shop. They have some fabulous carpets! There was a woman buying one. She had rotten taste! I told her the other one was much better for her. And there was this white one. It will look marvellous in the sitting room, just you wait."

"Oh yes," Mum thought, "with my family bringing in the garden on their feet!"

"Anyway, he's bringing it tomorrow. His name is Goldsmith. Can I drive?"

Mum looked round quickly, still no policeman.

"All right."

Mum excused herself by reckoning that driving was an activity, which would keep my mind occupied, if only on automatic pilot. It just might be safer than starting an argument. It was not till many years later that Alex drove her, under similar circumstances, straight into oncoming traffic, without appearing to see the significance. She wondered then if her reckoning had been at fault.

I drove safely home but insisted on making a detour to visit the "secret garden". This was a favourite haunt where someone, before the war, had planted exotic trees among which to build a house, but the house had never been built. It was a place of mystery where tranquillity was to be found. But not today.

I climbed over the fence gate and ran off. Mum, exhausted by the events of the day and the unknown fears, walked slowly up to the gate and leaned over it, calling after the retreating figure, "I'll wait here."

Presently, there being no answer, she called again: "Sal!"

"Coming!" The voice was further away. Much further.

"Sally, where are you? It's time to go home."

No answer.

Not knowing is in itself unnerving. Mum felt utterly spent, but the day was not over yet. And the night was to come.

In fact, I was not far off and soon came back when I thought of tea. Later, I was restless again and went out. I walked across the fields and came back to report that I had been talking with the horses. (I am not a person who has rapport with horses normally.) I had talked to them in their own language and we had all understood each other perfectly. There was a feathered serpent among their

13

number, which made Mum prick up her ears. Surely this was significant? Was there not a feathered serpent in the world of myths? I was now talking a great deal, as I had on that memorable journey to London. How was I ever going to sleep?

Mum dreaded the night. She gave me a double sleeping draught, having little hope that it would have any effect. She closed my door carefully and left her own open to hear the least movement. Sure enough, in the early hours I went along to the bathroom. Mum got up to open her own door so as not to miss the next move, and went back to bed, her ears skinned. Ten minutes passed and still no movement. I couldn't *still* be there? But I couldn't have come out without Mum hearing me? A few more minutes.

"What on earth can she be doing in there?" Mum was perplexed. "Squeezing her spots? Or practising her make-up or plucking her eyebrows?"

I couldn't be having a bath: Mum would have heard me. She must go and see.

The bathroom door was wide open, the room empty. Cold air was coming up the stairs. Mum went down. How had I managed to slip down so silently when Mum had heard me through the closed door when I first went down the passage? The front door was open. Oh no, I'd gone. Wasn't that just what Mum had hoped to forestall? Where had I gone? What would I do?

"And has she got any clothes on? More than likely not, in her present state of mind."

There was no answer to her call. Presently, she gave up and went to bed. She fell, belatedly, into a deep sleep, only to awaken with a leaden heart when the alarm went off.

She looked, without much hope, into my room, and went downstairs to start the day's chores by doing the grate in the sitting room. There, to her great surprise and relief, was me, curled up, fast asleep on the sofa. And I was wearing my nightdress. I remained sleeping for another hour, during which time the doctor was summoned. Had I been there all along? It took the rest of the morning to arrange for my admission to the local mental hospital, Graylingwell. Mum accompanied me and was allowed to stay for a while. If this sort of thing was going to keep on happening I may as well be cared for locally where Mum could visit daily and fit it in with jobs. She could ill afford the time and expense of London visiting on a regular basis. The glamour of that first admission to St. Thomas's had gone.

The Graylingwell treatment was to put me in a locked room with a mattress on the wooden floorboards and a bucket for excrement. The high shutters were barred shut. I would bounce on the mattress to try and see a glimmer of light at the top of the darkened window. The principle of the treatment was that I should have minimal stimulus until I simmered down. I was given Largactil, which made my tongue swollen and hard so I swore that would be a drug I would avoid for the rest of my life.

The whole exercise was very disappointing. Mum had hoped so much that I was on the ladder to success and here I was, back to square one. As we parted before I was taken down the corridor, I seemed quite cheerful, but Mum felt that this must be the end of the road. Or was it an endless circle? Pretty dismal, whichever way you look at it. She went home and made a cup of tea.

Her misery was interrupted by the telephone.

"Is that Mrs Dalglish?"

"It is."

"I'm glad I've found you at home. My name is Goldsmith."

Goldsmith? Goldsmith? Where had she heard that name? Oh Horror!

"Ah, Mr Goldsmith?"

"Yes, I've brought your carpet, but I'm lost. I've got as far as Harting. Can you tell me which road I should take from here?"

"Do you know, Mr Goldsmith, I am most awfully sorry but you have come on a false errand. I thought you would have realised that was not a genuine sale. It was my daughter who spoke to you. I have just this minute returned from taking her to Graylingwell."

Everyone knew what that meant. Mr Goldsmith retreated gracefully. Mum, on the point of tears when he rang, now burst out laughing. She laughed and laughed as if she could never stop.

Chapter 3

Cambridge

My first car was a Rover 75 with walnut dashboard and bucket seats, "the passion wagon". My long rust-coloured tweed coat, flared and fitted at the waist had been Mum's in the '50s. I sewed Gran's silver fox fur stole to the hem. It was no surprise that a letter addressed to "Sally, Chichester College" reached me.

Jewel Grant, our drama producer, who trained at RADA with Peter O'Toole and Albert Finney asked me to play Mrs Waters in *Tom Jones* and Lady India in *Ring Around the Moon*. People said I had charisma on stage. I gained distinction for "Vocational English Speaking". Fortnightly a girlfriend and I went to The Connaught Theatre, Worthing to see new plays. As social secretary at the college I invited The Who, who were extremely loud and smashed their instruments. For some reason I was given a special prize as the Student who contributed most to the Life of the College. In 1968 I was an usherette at Chichester Festival Theatre.

Studies went well and I was tutored for the Cambridge Entrance. On the day of the exam there was no invigilator available.

"Go to the back of the stage. Take this alarm clock and come back in three hours."

Not only was I disgruntled at being taken lightly, I had with me my briefcase full of notes on every aspect of humour, with examples.

The first question was: "A joke is a very serious thing."

The next: "Compare and contrast a poem by Dylan Thomas," with another I knew equally well.

I froze. I signed my name at the top and handed the papers back to the Head of English.

In the last minute scramble for university places I chose the one nearest to my father's farm: Bradford.

I drove the 300 miles there from Sussex on my newly acquired 50cc. scooter, stopping overnight in a pub. Knowing how hard it was going to be in new surroundings, Mum drove up with my trunk and helped me find suitable digs. We were fortunate to find a charming family, the parents both teachers who recently had decided not to take any more lodging students but were persuaded to make an exception for me. Mum felt comfortable that I would be well supported there. And so I was.

All went well for the first term and, to Mum's relief, I was welcomed back for a second term in the same digs. I too felt relief. It had taken all my determination to hold on for that first term, knowing that if I fluffed it, I would never get another chance. I made two friends: a computer science lecturer with shoulder length black hair and a Mech. Eng. Student with red hair who did the lighting for all the gigs. Feeling secure, I became somewhat carefree. It was fun to live "on a high". It made one very amusing and popular, because one could do and say things that other people would hesitate to do or say. On a high there are no inhibitions. It was like dancing on a tightrope, with all the confidence in the world. But it only needed one wobble.

Mum was to drive up from Sussex to pick me up on the way to Aunt D's cottage in Borrowdale where we were to spend Easter together. It was a bigger adventure than either of us had planned. Mum's car boiled over on the way, and thereafter she had to drive very slowly and keep stopping to fill up with water. At one of the stops she rang my digs to warn that she would be very late. The phone was answered by Maria who was in, alone.

"Is Sally there?"

"No, she's gone."

"Gone? But she's expecting me to pick her up. I'm just ringing to say I'm going to be late. Where is she?"

I don't know. She's not here any more."

18

"But where has she gone? How am I going to find her? What's happened? When did she go?"

"She came in very late last night, with a boyfriend. Daddy wouldn't let them in."

Bad as that! Mum could hardly blame him, he had a young family to protect and I was not his prime responsibility. There was a pause. Maria held on.

"Are you there, Maria? Where do you think she would have gone?

"You might try Dr MacLeod."

"All right, thank you. I'll do that."

Dr MacLeod, when Mum eventually puffed her way into Bradford, was concerned but could not help.

"Sally should have come for an injection this morning. Let's see?"

The notes revealed that I had not been in.

"I'm afraid I cannot help you. It's very sad. Such a charming girl. And wonderful company," he added with a smile.

"It is so tragic that one has to clamp down on her when she is having a good time. Whenever she is happy, one has to be afraid for her. It's so unfair."

It was getting late. No good going on to The Lake District now. Mum telephoned Charles, my eldest brother, who lived forty miles away with his wife, Carol. She hoped he would be able to mend the car. At about 10.00pm the phone rang.

"It's for you, Mother." Charles handed over the receiver.

"Is that Mrs Dalglish?"

"Yes.'

"Mrs M.K. Dalglish?"

"Yes."

"This is the police station at Cambridge. We have your daughter here and I'm wondering what to do with her."

"Oh! Thank heavens. I'll come straight away and collect her. Can you keep her till I come?"

"The welfare officer is on her way to see her. Will you wait till you hear from her?"

"Of course you can't go now: you must be worn out. Sal will be all right till the morning. You'd much better get a good night's sleep." Charles and Carol were adamant. And after half an hour, or so, the welfare officer rang to tell them that arrangements had been made to admit me to hospital. Mum promised to visit next day.

Good Friday. There was no time for a thorough examination of the car, but Charles took the radiator cap off and assured Mum that that would stop it behaving like a pressure cooker. The water would not boil away so quickly. Ever trustful Mum believed him and hoped for the best. She set off on her cross-country journey, on a road new to her, in heavy traffic, on a sorry mission. The weather was foul. But perhaps she should not have been grumbling. She had not gone many miles when the windscreen shattered.

Happy Easter! It might have happened on any other day, but on this, of all days, there could be no hope of replacement. With the glass fragments removed, she was reminded of the arctic conditions prevailing in her childhood motoring days. But then one catered for it with rugs and scarves, and even hot water bottles. Now, one expected to be warm while travelling and dressed accordingly.

She found a pleasant room for the night, and in the morning discovered me, in far the most attractive surroundings of their kind that we had yet been in. It was a purpose-built single storey building in cheerful, spacious grounds. Everyone seemed young, bright and happy: possibly because of its proximity to the university. And, of course, timing was important, as in St. Thomas's. What a marvellous place to be in! But for how long? Mum could not afford to linger and without her I would have no visitors. She felt that her visits were a lifeline to reality.

The tale came out. I had started walking at night and subsequently hitched a lift with an affable lorry driver who

20

said he was going to Cambridge. I thought of Professor Martin Ryle and how we used to play as children in his mother's cottage in Sussex. She had wagon wheel plaits round her ears. It seemed a good idea to go to Cambridge and look him up.

After being dropped off and wandering around I was hungry and my purse was empty. I approached a scholarly-looking man.

"Can you tell me where I can find Professor Martin Ryle?" I asked.

He turned, surprised. What could this wild-looking young woman want with Sir Martin Ryle on Good Friday evening? Or any other evening? I was curiously dressed and looked travel-stained, at least.

"Why do you ask?"

"I've come a very long way to see him."

He looked at me disbelieving.

"He's a friend of mine," I assured him.

"Mine too," he smiled, still disbelieving. "I tell you what, are you hungry?"

"Famished!" I answered.

"Then why don't we go and find something to eat?"

He could not have hit on a better idea.

"And do you know, Mum, he gave me black caviar!"

It was a sumptuous meal. He was probably as much surprised by my appetite as our conversation. The meal over, he delivered me to the police station to solve the rest of my problems.

Chapter 4

Teacher

It was about this time that great Aunt D died and left me one thousand pounds, which in 1971, was enough to buy me a back-to-back terrace house in Bradford. People on highs are apt to give away all their worldly goods to anyone who appears to be a worthy cause: at such times they are unlikely to be of sound judgment. So the timing of the bequest was doubly blessed, in that the money was tied up in unsquanderable property, and, henceforth I no longer risked being turned out of my digs, however reprehensible my behaviour. The mere ownership of my own home gave me a valuable sense of security and responsibility.

This was the year John France came into my life, probably the dearest friend I was ever to have. He came in stark contrast to the depraved life I had been living in Bradford. His mother, whom he adored, had died of cancer while he was in the Royal Navy, unable to obtain leave. As a Ship's Writer (librarian) he had a powerful, well-organised mind. He was largely self-educated and a natural student of life. Together we studied for my degree.

I was the leading lady in five of the seven plays we took to Edinburgh. The playwrights, director and actors loved to come to our house because John was witty, relaxed and such a great conversationalist. He'd have us playing "Chief Stoker" or entertain with his Fender guitar.

Despite a couple of breakdowns before John's appearance, I managed to get an Honours II.ii. Keen to do a postgraduate year in drama, I went to Bretton Hall with its beautiful lakes and peacocks. My accommodation was a Ford Transit, which John had converted for me. The course was intense. I lasted three weeks before sleep failed me.

John stuck by me and while he worked at Bingley College as a drama technician, I turned to waitressing, which I had done so many times in school holidays since I was fourteen. We both worked with a Gurdjieff group in Yorkshire whenever we could. They supported our idea of going overland to India. We had lived with different Asian families close by and wanted to see how they lived in their countries of origin. John had not only hand built a kitchen for the back-to-back terrace house, he had converted the attic and installed a bathroom in the single large bedroom. He made all the preparations for our mobile home in the Ford Transit. The aim was to go for a year, so we let a newly married couple rent the house.

Mum insisted on postcards every week, but was perturbed one week to get a letter from India describing how John had gone to buy gas one day. He had been gone four hours and returned eventually to say that he had been held up in the middle of a riot!

"But he's OK. We're enjoying ourselves."

Mum was worried. Ten days passed and she heard nothing more. At last, frantically she phoned the Foreign Office. She didn't know whether to hope for news or not. She explained her anxiety to a cheerful type at the other end.

"Oh, not to worry. We've heard nothing about them. You can take it that that means they're all right. We always hear at once if anyone winds up in prison or in hospital. They want to be paid!"

Somewhat dubiously reassured, Mum waited for the next move. She was living at The Folly, a four-bedroomed house she, Alex and a master builder had had great fun building in the Sussex woods. It wasn't long before John and I arrived on her doorstep, unannounced "as a surprise". The thread on the steering had gone and we had turned round to drive gingerly home. Despite all our adventures we felt that we had experienced the best of the Indian, Bangladesh and Pakistani cultures back in

Bradford. We had even been to a three-day wedding before our departure.

Feeling able to face anything together after our journey we decided to marry and three weeks later with just the playwright and the junk shop owner who'd sold me the house, for witnesses, we settled for a quiet wedding at the registry office. There were a lot of press and photographers because I'd put on a postcard: "Cinderella will be leaving her back-to-back on November 14th 1973 for her three-pound wedding." In contrast to Princess Anne leaving Buckingham Palace for her three-million pound wedding. I had won the Xandra Rhodes dress she wore the week before. On the day I wore my blue mini dress and white mac.

Managing the Bradford Work Centre for the Elderly set up by the Rotary Club was a challenge I enjoyed in 1974, but I still hankered to teach and embarked on a Postgraduate Certificate of Education at Bingley College. John primed me with dozens of questions I could ask on the teaching practice at a local Grammar School, and it was that school that remembered me and chose me over twenty-four other candidates for the post of English teacher.

Keeping order was not too much trouble as I lined the classes up outside the door until silent and inside placed the desks in square U's around my desk, to avoid the inevitable anonymity of the back row. I poured myself whole-heartedly into the work, both in preparation and scrutiny of essays, working habitually until 10.00pm, leaving little time for home-life, social life or even sleep.

A half-term trip with two teachers and a group of students to the Bay of Biscay was my undoing. I danced outrageously with the Swedish Chief Engineer and behaved irresponsibly. On return to school, taking Assembly, I replaced a hymn with "Bring Me Sunshine" and over the loud speakers omitted "the Kingdom" in the Lord's Prayer.

"Mrs France," the Welsh headmaster, Mr Farmer Little admonished, "that was very nearly sacrilege."

I grew more flamboyant; sleep suffered, and classes became hilarious. I returned to Lynfield Mount in Burley-in-Wharfedale. At least these days they realised that ECT did nothing for hypomanics: it was only beneficial for those with depression.

In the staffroom there were murmurings.

The headmaster addressed them: "Mrs France is one of my best teachers. I will not have a word said against her."

Sneers and jealousy were not easily squashed: "Does she think she knows more about teaching than some of us who have taught for years and know more about the job than she will ever learn?"

Mr Farmer Little welcomed me back, but it was tough going after a period of medication and hospitalisation.

In my third year at the school the pressure was mounting. It was a cold crisp January afternoon when I took the non-exam class to look for the Cottingley Fairies on the far side of the river.

"Miss, there isn't a bridge! We'll have to swim so we're not late for class!"

I took off my clothes and swam across the River Wharfe. Another boy took off most of his and swam behind me, rather close to the weir. The others scurried with our clothes round the thickets to where there was a small bridge and met us. Dressed I whipped into the hairdresser and said, "Adrian, can you just dry the ends and they'll never know where I've been."

By 2.00pm there wasn't one of the thousand pupils who did not know where I'd been. By this time we had a new headmaster, an impersonal man who was keen on bureaucracy. My resignation was called for, and awkward questions asked as to how I had managed to obtain a teaching position.

"If we had known that you had a history of mental illness, you would never have been recruited into the profession."

My pension fund contributions were cancelled and refunded. I was officially barred from teaching. What ignominy! Mum thought it was a tragic waste. She felt that if there were only a way to control my handicap I could have made a wonderful contribution to any teaching establishment.

To have the door so firmly and conclusively shut on my basic ambition was a terrible blow to my morale, to say nothing of the eclipse of our financial status. With my substantial income as a teacher, added to John's, we'd sold our terraced house in town and bought a double fronted mill house, the end of a row of back-to-backs, on the outskirts of town. This gave us space and a garden, a great source of joy for me, but a huge amount of work for John in the conversion to a single house. Since we were both working elsewhere the conversion was protracted and the ongoing state of chaos did nothing to promote a state of peace and relaxation, which we both needed. Maybe this was a contributory cause of my downfall. But we could not afford to pay workmen. John had made kitchen units in our other house and appeared to enjoy the challenge. Not much room for enjoyment now. In our despair, energy was at a premium. John gave up his job in order to work full-time on restoring the house to order. But the incentive had gone and work was as slow as ever. John's hope alighted on a second-hand printing press, a thing he'd always dreamed about. For some months he produced beautiful posters and business cards, until he was told by the Planners that the premises would have to have reinforced fire doors and floors. As if life were not difficult enough already!

Mum, at this time had come north to live with Alex, in his uninhabitable farmhouse. She was, therefore, able to visit me at home or in hospital. She was saddened to see what looked like a ruined life, regretting especially that in her view I had been such a responsible, generous child, putting a lot of personal energy into helping people less well off than myself. It did not seem fair to Mum that I had been reduced to this. I did not seem to know my own worth, or even my own identity, and no one could help.

A new psychiatrist said to me one day, "You know, Sally, the trouble with you is that you like being rude!"

As far as Mum could see, that hit the nail squarely on the head. Going over the border gave me a wonderful excuse to indulge in invective, and recriminations, which would have been totally unacceptable under normal conditions. Mum remembered the early days when I criticised her ruthlessly for letting the family break up, and consequently my breakdowns. Mum was convinced then that I could not help myself and was not to be blamed for my cruelty. Even now I couldn't see how I could help going over the border when the time came and the pressure was irresistible.

I procured a job as a waitress in the private executive's dining room at Rank Hi Fi, dressed to the nines in stilettos and waistcoat, and did flower arrangements for their table. I organised wine tastings with Mr Russell the manager of the Wharfedale speaker department. He taught me how to drink ground coffee black without sugar. I usually waited demurely to attend my clients or their guests. Although the room was often filled with flowers, the managers noticed no difference from previous days until they began to discuss the relative merits of Yorkshire and Lancashire.

"You're both wrong!" came an unexpected voice. "Sussex is better than either!"

The look of astonishment on every face was worth seeing. When he had recovered his wind, the chairman spoke: "But you are not included in this conversation!"

Perhaps not. But I soon was. It was not long before visiting potentates were introduced to me.

"This is Sally. She looks after us. She's all right if you keep on the right side of her."

One of their members failed once to take that elementary precaution. He asked one day why the soup was always thick?

"I don't know," I said. "I expect it's because it comes out of packets and they don't make it. Would you like some consommé?"

"I would very much," replied Dr Marsh.

"I'll make you some myself," I promised.

Delighted to have a chance to show my prowess, I put a turkey carcass from the canteen into the pressure cooker with carrots and onions and mixed the resulting liquid with elderflower champagne. Nellie, the cook, showed me how to clarify the liquid by whisking in egg whites and shells and straining it. Mr Russell and Dr Marsh both ordered consommé, but Dr Marsh was engrossed and said not a word. His colleague whispered a discreet, "The soup was delicious," but my fury lasted next day when I reached for the Bisto and presented a bowl of it to the offender.

"Oh, Sally, I forgot to say how much I enjoyed your soup yesterday!"

"Too late!" I retorted. "You've got gravy today."

At home there was no serenity, no certainty. John rang Mum one day to ask if she would come and stay the night, for he was exhausted and had had no sleep the night before. Glad to be asked, Mum knew only too well what this meant: I had not been sleeping. It was unlikely that anyone would get any sleep that night. When I reached that point there seemed to be nothing anyone could do to restore things. But John and I refused to be beaten and were attempting the impossible to prevent me from having to admit one more failure.

It was a Friday evening; the doctor had gone away for the weekend, and John had persuaded him that he could contain the situation over the weekend. Clearly he could not, even with Mum's help. At last they gave up trying, and persuaded me to accompany them in the car. But when we reached the hospital, I had changed my mind and refused to get out of the car. They sat for a quarter of an hour trying to tempt me out with this ruse or that, but to no avail. Mum tried a new tack.

"I'm going to see if I can get any tea." She opened the car door and alighted.

"Good idea," I said at once. "I'll come with you."

After that it was simple. I knew the way up to the ward. We reached sister's office and were greeted and asked to take a seat. Waiting is never easy under such circumstances. Everyone seemed to be very busy. Sister was on the phone. Doctors came and went; patients wandered in and out. I looked more and more like a pressure cooker about to blow off.

Mum called a nurse, "Can't anybody do anything about her? Can't they see she's getting steamed up?"

"It is because they can't find her own doctor. She has to be certified."

"I lured her in with the hope of a cup of tea," Mum murmured. The nurse beamed. I'll get you one at once." She quickly brought a tray with three cups and some biscuits, which eased the situation.

At last the doctor, red tape concluded came up to me and said affably, "Hallo Sally, how are you today?"

The safety valve was about to blow. I drew myself up to my very considerable height in my long black coat and took a deep breath. I appeared to tower over the doctor. Perhaps they all shrank a little.

"How DARE you ask how I am?"

Fury leapt like a flame from my eyes. Sister went to the telephone again.

"Come now, Sally," the doctor tried to keep his composure, but I had not finished with him.

"You have the IMPERTINANCE to ask me how I am. You know well how I am! And you keep me waiting here. Well, I'll tell you how I am. And I'll tell you what I think of you and your hospital."

I proceeded to do just that, in full un-expurgated measure – glorious technicolour, one might almost say. Mum had heard such language before, so the shock to her modesty as not new. She wondered if John had, and if he thought that was the way she had brought me up.

29

I had noted sister's move to the phone and interpreted it correctly. I moved over to the door while delivering my diatribe and sat down purposefully in front of it, leaning comfortably against it, so that when the knock came, the answer had to be:

"Wait a minute, please."

Presently I ran out of words, and ended with a very loud roar. Silence followed. I was the only one who was completely at ease. What next? *Fools step in where angels fear to tread.* No one spoke. At last Mum, with the same intuition that had led her to suggest tea, now remembered my love of drama.

"You must feel a lot better with that off your chest?"

Delighted, I burst into laughter. "Oh," I said helplessly, "that was *good,* wasn't it?"

I was led away, quietly and happily, while Mum and John were taken to wait in another office. There the doctor came to tell them that I was asleep.

"It usually takes six men to hold her down for an injection."

Chapter 5

John Peel Byre

Once more I returned home and took up the threads of life. But the foundations were shaken. John was a disillusioned man. He was a problem-solver who would help anyone. As an idealist he had imagined that he could cure me, but the demon always returned to the attack. Our marriage had seemed a strong one and John worried most about the example it would set to our friends if we were to part. He had reached a point of despair fearing that he too might "go round the bend". Our friends thought it possible and were deeply concerned for us both. They recommended that it was time John took care of himself. And what about me? John was in torment. I went high again, once more on a weekend. John was reluctant to call the doctor. Mr Russell, to whom I had turned as a father figure for help, took me back to his wife. Together we decorated the church for the harvest festival. Good Methodists that they were, they took care of me all day, like a daughter, treating me to the best Gewürztraminer for lunch. In the evening John rang Mum asking her to take me away for a spell next day.

When Mum came, it was obvious that I was heading for hospital once more, after the inevitable sleepless night. But it was always worth trying to avoid that extremity. She did not really want to take me to Ruthwaite and expose the family troubles to her new-found "happy family" hamlet, where nobody knew anything more about her than she cared to tell them. Instead, she decided to take me to the Lakeland cottage for which she could pick up the key, and which was familiar to me.

We talked and we walked in the old holiday haunts, and Mum fancied that all might be well. But the nights are always impossible in such circumstances. It was 2.00 in the morning when Mum woke up, feeling that something was wrong. My door was open. The front door was open. How had I managed to get down those stairs, when every board creaked a warning? And where on earth had I got to now? Mum groaned. I might have gone down the road, to lean over the bridge, a favourite spot, but not likely to be entertaining at night. There was a moon, but it was cloudy. If Mum followed me down the road, I might just as easily have gone up the road. But where to? She'd better stay put, to greet me if and when I came back. Mum stood uncertain, by the open door. In the stillness of the night she could hear voices. Odd, at this hour? Not voices, but one voice. One unmistakable voice rose to the pitch of a tub-thumper at Hyde Park Corner. It came from inside the hotel, further up the road on the other side.

Mum put on her outdoor shoes and, girding up her dressing gown, strode purposefully up the road and rang the bell, at the hotel entrance. Nothing happened. She rang again: still nothing. The moon was hiding behind a cloud, but she made her way through the little garden gate, and stumbled round to the back. That was much livelier. The lights were on, and the door open. The voice was loud and clear. Nobody came to the door, so she went in, and met the landlord in his dressing gown.

"I think you've got my daughter here?"

"Yes, indeed." He was thankful to see her, and led her up the backstairs to where I was holding forth. I looked extremely comfortable, sitting on the staircase, leaning against the wall, in my nightdress (thank heaven, Mum breathed) and slippers. I was surrounded by a fascinated audience in various states of disarray, including the helpless manager, who would have liked to break the party up, but didn't know how. Mum joined the audience. No one moved. I continued my harangue. Presently, Mum suggested quietly, "Perhaps, if you would all go back to bed, she might come home with me?"

The manager lingered; after all, it was his place. He felt responsible.

"You too, if you don't mind?"

Left alone, mother and daughter had a few words before I agreed to go home. Mum was determined that I should sleep for the rest of the night, and accordingly gave me five of her own sleeping tablets. There was another hotel further up the road, and she was taking no chances. One tablet was the normal dose; two made her feel ill the next day; but she knew that people who were severely disturbed could tolerate huge doses, sometimes without any apparent effect. Five was a guess, possibly a dangerous one. But what doctor could she call, at this time of night? And what doctor knew the answer, anyway?

As it happened, the guess was about right. I slept till 7.30am. By that time Mum was ready to take me back to John, and to hospital. Leaving me sadly but safely tucked up on a ward, Mum went to talk to John. She felt enormously sorry for him. He was such a good, kind man. He had been a remarkable support to me through my degree studies, the teacher training and the actual teaching. His efforts had been monumental, seeing me through so many crises, never till now, losing heart. He was largely responsible for what success had been ours.

"John," Mum said, "we all owe you a tremendous debt for what you have done for Sal. I shall always look on you as a son. But has it occurred to you that if you leave her in hospital now, she might never come out again?"

It was a harsh thing to say to a broken man. No one knew for sure how I would react, but Mum was sure that many, if not all people who fill our vast mental hospitals, are there, simply because they have been abandoned by their loved ones. I had told her that once, when she visited me "inside".

Tears filled John's eyes as he replied, "I've thought about that. I know it's possible. But I can't go on any longer."

Mum tried to comfort him.

"You're such a good man, John. I'll go and see her and take her home with me when she is ready to come."

In the event I came speedily out of hospital, eager to start a new life, masking the deepest sadness I felt in letting go of the man I cherished. Mum thought I might be able to run my own little restaurant if we could refurbish John Peel Byre, which was joined to John Peel's Cottage. She let the upper part of the building to holiday guests. The idea was immediately appealing. Throughout the winter we were dreaming and scheming, and actually helped to build the extension, learning many new skills and forgetting old troubles. The builder was the son of the farmer across the road, and his mate lived next door. Both were immeasurably kind and patient with their amateur, bumbling "help", and made the whole adventure huge fun. The neighbours were all friendly, and provided me with a variety of company, which I always found essential.

When the building was finished and decorated, complete with Honister slate fireplace, there was the furnishing, a fresh excitement. We used some of Aunt D's old oak tables, an octagonal gate leg and some smaller round tables. Her willow pattern china and silver cutlery would add elegance. We took the car to furniture auctions to buy sixteen more or less matching chairs. At one sale, a carpet that might normally have been three hundred pounds, we bought for a mere fifteen pounds. Velvet curtains were plentiful and we managed to get a pair just the right size. Perhaps the best value was the additional china, cutlery and glasses for under thirty pounds. The bank manager was not greatly inconvenienced.

Every month Mum and I went south to visit Dandan, my grandmother, which Mum had always done since she moved north. The spare room was occupied by Alex, who worked eighty-four hours a week for alternate weeks at The Sanitorium. We enjoyed the chance to see him too. We had brought a camp bed for me to sleep on in the box rom. Mum slept on the sofa. We paid our last visit in April, before Easter opened the holiday season. Once the season started we would not be able to leave the restaurant until it closed. We explained all this to Dandan and promised to come again in September.

Dandan, at ninety-three, had her life extremely well organised. She had moved six years previously, when her driving license expired, under her own steam, despite the efforts of trustees to interfere, leaving the big house with panoramic views and a lengthy drive. She now lived in a small bungalow in the centre of the village, surrounded by a great number of friends, of whom she was the uncrowned queen. A gardener came once a week; her groceries were delivered, post and paper, of course, and meals-on-wheels. She enjoyed these because of the "nice women" who brought them. The meals were mostly distributed to the birds.

She thrived on a self-devised diet of bananas for breakfast, with strong coffee and toast; a glass of Dubonnet mid-morning; digestive biscuits and cheese for lunch with perhaps a sample of the "bird food" and stewed apple with a baked custard for supper. The baked custard was put in the oven at an exact hour, and removed when due to be eaten. The stewed apple was cooked in a shallow saucepan with sugar and water until the smell reached her in the next room. By that time half of its contents had boiled over and settled into a sticky, gradually blackening, and undetected layer of toffee below the burner. It was not until later that the absence of a thermostat was discovered, when Mum, undertaking to make the custard, and forgetting to take it out on time, retrieved it later in the form of a cinder. The suggested addition was quite unnecessary.

"My custards are always perfect! You can't cook, that's all."

Perhaps the crowning glory of her present existence was her grandson, who had moved in with her. Not for *her* convenience. She did not need anyone and would stoutly have resisted any suggestion that she did. But Alex had recently taken a live-in job as night porter at the King

Edward VII Hospital. A strange job, some thought, but it had the advantage that he would be near friends; that he could do his pastels and pen and inks in the small hours when the switchboard was quiet, and that he could dash up to Lancashire on alternate weeks to work on his farmhouse. He would also be able to keep a surreptitious eye on his grandmother, thereby relieving his mother's conscience. At the same time her garage held attractions for his bangers. He shared this fun with Dandan, taking her out for a spin in each new acquisition, even taking her riding side-saddle on the pillion of his motorbike, as in the days of her youth she had ridden on ponies. At eighty-seven it was still important to her to be surrounded by men, so it was the easiest thing in the world, when he found it too noisy in the hospital to sleep by day, to move in with Dandan.

Nevertheless, there were limits. No one was going to take advantage of Dandan and get away with it. Alex told Mum one day that he thought he might set up his paintings on the dining room table, which was never used. Dandan always ate off the trolley, and so too did anyone who came, so there was that tempting space with an artist's dream of a northern window by it. Mum thought it a great idea and mentioned it tentatively to Dandan.

"What!" said the old lady, in astonishment. "Leave his mess on my table? Certainly not!"

However, next time Mum visited she noticed the changed outlay, to Alex's entire satisfaction, with no complaints. The two of them understood each other pretty well. He did a dozen portraits of Dandan's beloved brother, George Mallory and many other close copies of Rembrandt, Van Gogh and dignitaries that lined the hospital walls. His numerous pastel landscapes were atmospheric.

He kept an old Rover 3000 to take him comfortably to Lancashire and a series of A40s with interchangeable parts for getting to work.

A puzzled admirer of Dandan's asked indignantly one day, "Why does he have to park his old wreck just outside her window where it spoils her view?"

"Because it is his pride and joy," Mum laughed. "They both love it!"

No one else could have got away with it. But Alex gave her a chance to remember something of her madcap youth. She could afford this measure of disrepute, and reveled in it.

Meanwhile, Mum and I tried to drum up business for the John Peel Byre restaurant. It was a simple menu of homemade steak pie, Cumberland sausage and so on. No license, so customers were charged three-pound "corkage" and brought their own drinks. The Look North news team would come across from Carlisle, ordering their curries of choice the night before. I knew my Pakistani warehouses, so would speed off to Bradford in the early morning to buy the fresh spices for either the vegetarian dish Anna Ford had ordered or a Rogan Josh. Mum helped grinding spices and preparing starters. She was a fast worker and never too tired for the washing up.

The holiday visitors and some of the neighbours came but it was a venture we did not take too seriously with regard to planning permission, fire regulations, food regulations and all the other regulations that might need to be satisfied.

Several people gave me special orders, such as a young Austrian couple commissioning a meal for three, to include me. This was to comprise wild watercress soup, T-bone steaks and Apfelstrudel. I was given careful instructions about the dessert and duly laid the filo pastry on a cotton sheet on the octagonal table, covered it with ingredients, and then grabbed two corners to roll it before placing it like a snake on a baking tray. The butcher told me how to guarantee mouth-watering steaks. The Apfelstrudel?

"My father makes this every week." How could I compete?

The restaurant was never without customers. Probably the times when it was not full were the best as I could talk to the guests, which I loved.

"It seems a pity I can't advertise. It might be courting trouble."

Friends suggested, "Why not put a placard at the end of the road."

That seemed innocuous enough. The cottage was in a cul-de-sac leading from a lane to nowhere. If it attracted one extra family occasionally, it would be worth it. I painted a simple message in white paint on green slate: Evening Meals, 7.30. John Peel Byre.

Two days later, on returning from our walk, we were greeted by the news, "Somebody's been looking for you."

"Oh. Do you know who?"

"It looked like the Council! They took a jolly good look."

They might as have well said: the Gestapo.

"I wish I hadn't laid the tables." I kicked myself.

"You didn't think to draw the curtains?" Of course not, we'd been feeling safe. Was it the new notice? Or was it a routine snoop? Or both?

"You wouldn't think these little lanes worth patrolling for criminality."

The next day's post confirmed our fears. Mum received a letter purporting to come from the chairman of the special planning board:

Dear Madam,

It has been reported to me, by one of my inspectors, that you have placed a notice on the public highway, advertising provision of meals to the public. You do not have permission for this activity, and I must ask you to remove the notice in question, immediately. Furthermore, you may not serve meals to the public without permission.

38

Mum found some satisfaction in replying:

Dear Sir,

With regard to your instructions, may I say that it is no hardship to comply in the matter of the notice. It was never likely to do us much good; in fact, the only eye it caught was that of your inspector. But..." and she went on to explain the circumstances.

She was rewarded by gracious permission to carry on, subject to limitations: no advertising. So nothing was lost. This was really about the scale of operations that we could manage comfortably. The season progressed happily enough, until July.

Chapter 6

The Bungalow

Dandan could really be said to have got life taped. Not only did she have Alex in attendance, many friends to visit her whom she could walk to visit, but one of her sons and family were nearby. There was one particular admirer who kept an eye on her from a safe distance. He passed her window every morning to make sure she was all right, averting his eyes. Only occasionally would he call in for a chat.

But this was not enough. Mum had not been down to see her lately. Why not? She quite forgot that she could not come down until September. Nothing was important enough to keep her away. It was her duty to come. She didn't discuss the matter with anyone. She was never one for the direct approach.

Alex rang one evening to tell Mum that the old lady had had a fall and cut her shin. It had been seen to all right, but he was unnerved and the neighbours were fussing, saying that at her age she should have someone with her all the time. It was too big a responsibility. Alex wondered whether he should give up his job to be with her. Mum was indignant.

"That's absurd!" she said. "You've got all your life in front of you. I quite see that it would be difficult for you to pull out now, if you wanted to, but if Dandan has reached the stage when she needs someone to look after her, it is my job. I promised her years ago that as long as she kept out of hospital, I would look after her till she died in her own home."

"She's all right at the moment, and she's walking around with her stick. But what happens if she does it again?"

"Surely she'll take care not to!"

"Do you think you ought to come down?"

"Quite honestly, Al, I can't see any point. She's had a fall, and been picked up again. There's not a lot I could do if I did come. And I really don't think I should leave Sal on her own. Apart from anything else, she couldn't manage without my back up in the restaurant. I did explain that to Dandan."

Dandan was not pleased. Dash it! It had not worked: she fell again. Not so painfully this time, but enough to infer that it might become a habit. Panic stations! Alex rang Mum again.

"I hate to tell you but she's done it again!"

"Oh dear, then I *must* come, somehow."

Mum did not at all like leaving me, but I assured her that I would be perfectly all right and found a volunteer to take her place at the sink. Obviously, Mum must go.

She found Dandan gracious in her triumph, not suffering unduly, but during the night heard her call in a querulous voice, as one who would say, "Where on earth have you been and why didn't you come sooner?" She rushed to her mother's room and found her on the floor, unhurt.

"Oh, there you are," said Dandan. "Where am I?"

"You seem to have fallen out of bed. Are you all right?"

"Yes, I'm all right."

Mum put her back to bed and straightened the covers.

In the morning Dandan had no recollection of the incident. However, Mum took it to be an acknowledgement of the fact that the time had come for her to honour her promise. This was the moment Mum had always dreaded. She knew well that the only reason for her existence, in her mother's estimation, was as an insurance policy against Dandan's old age. She knew, too, that she would only be called upon as a last resort, since Dandan had no intention of yielding sovereignty to anyone.

Knowing this, she yet failed to recognise the current situation.

"Mother," she said before the end of her visit, "we are all very worried about you, falling over like this. I think it is time I came to look after you. Alex can't look after you when he's at work or asleep."

"It's very nice to have you here; I've missed you."

"The only trouble is, as I told you, I can't leave Sal. I should not really have left her now, but your need seemed more urgent. I have to go back to her now, but the season will be finished in a month's time, and then we can pack up and come and live with you."

"What is Sally doing now?"

"She's running her little restaurant, do you remember? We added a kitchen and dining room beyond John Peel's cottage where she makes evening meals for visitors."

Dandan was not especially interested, her mind probably working on the phrase, "in a month's time". If she needed Mum now, she needed her NOW. Why wait for a month?

Mum completed her four hundred-mile journey next day and was relieved to find that I had got on very well in her absence. She had hardly got into the house when the phone rang.

"I hate to tell you…"

"I know, don't tell me! She's done it again."

"How did you guess?"

"I haven't been your grandmother's daughter for seventy years for nothing. She's won again! She always does. I feel like swearing, but there's nothing I can do about it. If I call her bluff, she knows darned well that she has the whip hand, and that I would not abandon her."

"So, what are you going to do about it?"

"There's only one thing I can do. I'll abandon ship here and be along in a couple of days."

I was disappointed because I had begun to stand on my own feet. I was having fun in my restaurant, having attracted a lively group of young people who were stimulating and happy enough to include me in their discussions and parties.

"I'm sorry, darling, really I am. In fact, I am sick as mud! But apart from Dandan's needs and my duty, the winter was going to be a bit of a problem here. Some of your friends are leaving the area, and when the visitors are all gone, it is going to be rather lonely here. Last year it was all right because we had the excitement of building. This year there'd be nothing to do."

Loneliness, I had to admit, was something I could do without. Perhaps, after all, it would be fun to settle down near my old childhood haunts in Sussex. There must be plenty of people around with whom I went to Primary School. It might not be too bad.

There were no bookings so it was a simple enough to close down the business. If I were to settle down south it seemed best to take as much of my worldly personal belongings as possible. An unsettled state was as bad as a lonely one. I must try and establish a new root as soon as possible; the present one was insecure as long as Dandan's pull to the south claimed Mum's allegiance. So the little car groaned once more, this time without the benefit of hope.

Alex greeted them on arrival. Mum, still smarting, was churlish: "Dandan just couldn't wait, could she? How is it she always manages to create the maximum inconvenience?" Mum wished she had not spoiled the pleasure of seeing Alex again.

Dandan was delighted to see them. She had won, as she knew she would. The fact that there was no room for either of them, and no preparations had been made for their arrival mattered not at all. They were women weren't they? They could find room somewhere. And it would be nice not to have to get her own supper, now that they were here.

The main bedroom was, of course, Dandan's. The spare room was overflowing with Alex's things. The tiny box room was full of assorted junk. It measured 6' by 6'6'. If that cupboard were taken out, space could be made for the camp bed that they had brought with them. There was no room for it in the garage, with all Al's paraphernalia, so it had to be left out in the garden. It didn't occur to anyone that there was plenty of room in Dandan's room. That was sacrosanct. With the camp bed installed, leaving room for the door to open, there was room for precious little else. My boxes were piled high in the unused end of the living room. When that space was filled Alex and I looked further afield and spotted Dandan's wardrobe. Plenty of room there: Dandan would never even notice if we put a couple of boxes up there.

We were wrong, of course.

"I hardly feel the house is my own any more," she said wistfully when next she went to bed and saw them. She had probably heard us going into her room. The boxes were removed forthwith and put in the banished cupboard in the garden. Mum had brought only an overnight case and a duvet. She was able to curl up on the sofa at night and remove all traces of her invasion by hiding her bag and bedclothes behind the bookcase by day. She had stayed with Dandan once before, when lending The Folly to Simon and his bride. Mum had made herself practically invisible, with the result that Dandan had pronounced the visit "a great success".

Alex handed in his notice. I took on the cooking. Mum began to make plans for some sort of occupation. When Alex had vacated the garage they could try restoring furniture. They toured the junk shops on a round of inspection. Of course, they could not actually do anything yet, but it was nice to be ready. The cleaning lady turned up one morning and was told: "My daughter has come to look after me now; I shan't need you any more."

The "nice women" were dispatched. She could hardly expect them to come merely to feed the birds when Dandan had a resident cook. I did my level best to tempt Dandan's appetite, but the truth was that she preferred her own diet. The glamour of having all her family in thrall, was beginning to wear a little thin. Why didn't Mum and I go home now? We'd paid our visit. That was all that was required of us. Had she forgotten that we, instead of Alex, were going to look after her?

Mum heard her telling a friend who asked, "How long are they staying?"

"I don't know."

"We've come to look after you, Mother. You sent for us, don't you remember? Sal and I are going to stay with you now, so that Alex can go and finish working on his house in Lancashire."

Dandan looked vacant.

"You need someone to live with you in case you fall again. Al can't keep an eye on you and work at the same time."

Dandan kept her composure, but the enormity of what was happening began to dawn on her. This was not what she had planned at all. Life with Alex suited her admirably. Something about him reminded him of her brother, George. She liked to know that Mum was available should she need her. She certainly didn't want her in sight or underfoot day in, day out. She was quite fond of me. We played great games of Bezique together and made each other laugh. But she didn't want me interfering with her routines. In fact, there was no call for either of us at this time. And what was this about Alex going away? It was unthinkable.

"Yes, Dandan, you knew I was going when Mum and Sal came. It's time I set to work in earnest on my old farmhouse. It's taking forever."

"No, I didn't know."

"There isn't room for all of us, you see."

"But *you* mustn't go! I can't spare you!" she smiled mischievously, making a joke of it.

"Sorry, Dandan, but I must. They've come now, with all Sal's things. And you know I couldn't look after you properly. If you keep falling down, someone has to be around to pick you up again."

Dandan smiled wryly. Maybe all was not lost yet.

The following morning she did not look very well. In fact, she looked very ill indeed. Near to death's door in fact? We were all thoroughly alarmed. The doctor was sent for and brandy administered. Dandan had pulled a face over it, so it was not that that was the explanation, Mum thought uncharitably.

"Dubonnet," murmured Dandan, as the doctor took her blood pressure.

"Yes," said the doctor, "give her a sip of Dubonnet when she wants it and give her something light to eat when she's ready for it. Let me know if you are worried about her. Good morning."

Dandan looked frail, lying there with her eyes closed in a frown. She was trying to say something – "Light." At last Mum understood that there was a small chink of light, at the corner of the curtain, which was giving offence. She drew the curtain more tightly and the frown left Dandan's face. Mum tiptoed out to rejoin us.

Alex was saying, "I'll have to ask them to take my notice back."

"Then we can go back to John Peel's cottage," I added expectantly.

Mum joined in, "It's not as simple as that. You may not get your job back. And if you do, there's nowhere for us all to squeeze in here for any length of time."

"Why can't you go back?"

"What, now we've closed down just before the end of the season and brought all Sal's things down here? And if we did go back, there's no knowing when it might happen all over again. We can't come up and down, four hundred miles at a time, like a yo-yo."

"Well, I'm sorry for poor old Dandan. She's been jolly good to me and I'm very fond of her. I can't leave her now if it's going to kill her."

"Well, *we* can't go," Mum said. "She's got us on the end of a string, and she's ruthless enough to jerk it whenever she fancies."

Alex was shocked. It was not decent to speak so of the so nearly dead. There was no cause for such bitterness. I, on the other hand, knew something of my mother's frustration.

"I'll go and see if she wants anything," I volunteered.

Alex telephoned the hospital to see if he could have his job back. It had already been advertised under rather different conditions than had applied to him. Instead of doing straight nights, some early shifts and some late, it was now proposed that the night porter should work seven twelve-hour shifts on end, followed by seven nights off duty. Alex was surprised. This was what he had always begged them to do, so that he would have time to work alternate weeks on his farmhouse and yet collect two weeks' pay for the one on/one off. He was a bit hurt that they should decide to work this pattern only after he had resigned. But he re-applied, as requested, and was delighted to find that the job was his once more.

Dandan waited only to be sure of his success to make a full recovery. Her triumph would have been complete, no doubt, if she could have got rid of those women, to be replaced perhaps by the "nice women" and Mrs Mopp. But Mum and I were not easily to be shaken off. When the inevitability of the situation became apparent, Mum decided that it would be safe to leave the three of us to look after each other while she escaped to fetch some clothes.

"Dandan needs a housekeeper," she announced, "and Sal needs a job. There's no room for me here, and I'm afraid I don't contribute much to the joy of the household! So I'm going to take myself back to John Peel's cottage, get some clothes and generally tidy up there. We shall have to sell it before we can look for any sort of extra accommodation around here. You'll be all right, won't you? You can always ring me if you need me. In fact, I may as well stay there for the present."

Mum felt a bit of a heel, opting out like this but felt that we must agree that we would be better off without her.

With a huge sigh of relief she left us to it. Alex had always been a huge support to me and would let Mum know if there was any need to feel anxious. In any case, the local hospital was familiar to me and I had friends around. As for Dandan, she could only be thankful to see the back of Mum, who was beginning to be tiresome.

Alex was rather relieved not to have to return to his lonely old farmhouse permanently, but to be able to go up every other week was encouraging. He and I got on well together.

In the morning I might spend hours making something especially seductive but when lunchtime came Dandan was heavily asleep, having demanded an extra glass of Dubonnet. It was frustrating until I gave up trying to change her ways and let her see to her lighter lunch. Since looking after Dandan was pretty undemanding, I took on the maintenance of six gardens, mostly by word of mouth through Dandan's friends. My employers were diverse and interesting, and each of their gardens on a different soil from chalk to greensand. The local boys' college and members of the village had a thriving Gilbert and Sullivan society. I attended rehearsals, feeling somewhat aware of my status as a divorced woman. One night we rehearsed late and I returned about eleven o'clock. I crept past Dandan's door.

"Sally, is that you?"

I opened her door and put my head round the corner.

"Sorry, Dandan. I didn't mean to wake you."

"You didn't wake me," said Dandan sternly. "I have not been to sleep. I'm very disappointed in you, Sally. It is past eleven o'clock. Your bedtime is ten o'clock. It is most disappointing that I cannot trust you to keep good time. You may go to your room now."

Flabbergasted, I turned to go.

"Good night, Dandan," I said faintly.

"Good night, Sally."

But I'm a married woman, or I was, not a ten-year old for whom she's responsible! Come to think of it, it is I who am responsible for her! How can she treat me like this? This is stupid! She's not going to stop me going out if I want to. I could go to bed at one o'clock when I was married. I suddenly missed John. Why did we ever part company? Marriage couldn't have been as bad as this! I rang him up and he comforted me but did not suggest, or allow me to suggest meeting up with him again.

This ménage staggered on for some months. Mum revelling in her escape, holding her breath for fear of recall, was to have come down for Christmas, but was prevented by snow. I put my best efforts into making the occasion festive for Dandan and Alex. Alex was happy enough. He always had the doctors and patients to return to and the nurses doted on him, writing to him from faraway places when they were not nursing. Dandan, the centre of much attention, was content. Mum decided that she was dispensable enough to snatch a visit to her grandchildren in Australia, while she still could. She bought a ticket for a return in April, and, for the first time, insured against cancellation.

She paid a visit to us, hoping that Alex would be able to take her to Heathrow but found us in less good shape than we had led her to believe and felt guilty.

"If you could find somewhere near here, Mum, so that I could get away sometimes, it would make all the difference," I told her.

"Yes, I'm sorry, you've borne all the brunt of it. But at least I've been able to put John Peel Cottage to rights, so that it can be let in our absence. And I promise you, I'll look for some sort of root round here as soon as I get back. In fact, you'd better start looking for me, to save time."

With that, Mum bid us a cheerful farewell and put the width of the world between herself and our troubles. There is nothing like distance for relieving the pressure. She had a superb holiday and came back utterly refreshed. It was just as well. Alex and I were there to meet her at the airport. We were thrilled. Not only were we genuinely pleased to see her back, I was longing to tell her how I had

49

spent my first gardening money on an oriental rug with a hole in it. Through friends I had tracked down a Persian rug restorer who, in exchange for my designing him a shrubbery and tending his roses, was willing to teach me how to clean and repair oriental rugs. At the same time, the Weavers Group in Graffham had allowed me to join their weaving classes and offered me the Weavers' cottage for the price of the heating.

"I'm going to move in straight away. Isn't that lovely?"

Mum, though taken aback, said, "Well done! You deserve it, my dear! Though I must admit, it's a bit of a shock. I thought it was I who was going to find an extra roof? What are you going to live on?"

"Don't worry, Mum, I can still fit in all the gardening. And I'm going to be cleaning and mending rugs for people."

Mum felt that I had done more than my share in taking on a job that was rightfully hers. She listened with foreboding to our tales of exasperation and hopes of better things to come. From this moment Dandan was all hers. For two years they were hardly out of each other's sight.

Dandan affected a not-quite-with-it air.

"Are you going to sell John Peel's cottage?"

"Yes, I'm afraid I'll have to, if I can."

"Do you want to sell it?"

This, over and over again, until the answer came through clenched teeth.

"No, I don't at all want to sell it. But what else can I do?"

"Do you want to sell it?"

In any case, it was unsalable, and if she had found a buyer, it would only have yielded half the value of southern accommodation. All the hopes and dreams of space remained impossible. Dandan remained in possession of her spacious bedroom. Alex occupied fully, the spare room. I had insisted on the purchase of a full sized single bed to replace the camp bed. This had two big drawers, which solved the furniture problem in that room.

The kitchen was too small for a chair, and in the living room Dandan presided all day in her winged chair by the bay window. There was a matching chair the other side, sharing the view to the South Downs; a third fireside chair, for visitors, and four dining room chairs round the table at the other end of the room. The only available seat in the house, outside the sitting room, was the lavatory.

There was nowhere to do anything, and not much to do. Dandan hated the "barge barge" of the vacuum cleaner, and it had to be used in the very short space of time when she was absent from the room. There was a minimum of cooking required, but that little, in the middle of the day, Mum felt, precluded the possibility of taking a job. I used to do different gardens morning and afternoon. In the afternoons, Mum would take Dandan out for runs in the car, sometimes visiting Dandan's friends; sometimes just "petrol burning". They had favourite spots, where Mum would stop the car, and they would sit and admire a change of view. Sometimes Dandan would refuse to go. She would do this, in the early days, by way of protest, at her loss of independence. She was never known to complain of her lot, but her powers of communication were subtle and all pervasive. No one was in any doubt as to what she felt. Those feelings had always resulted in the satisfaction of her will.

Now, for perhaps the first time in her life, her will was challenged. She didn't want Mum here particularly, but she was still here, and not even at her sole command. It was small wonder she was morose.

Mum, one day, noticed an advertisement in the Daily Telegraph for a writing school. Now there was something she had always wanted to do, and never had time for! It was the perfect answer to her problems. As an occupation, it would take up no space; she could be available for service when required. And it need not even make a noise. When she wanted to type, she could sit on her bed, and anyway, Dandan was so deaf that she could never hear anything Mum said, so she might not even hear the typewriter. (Mind you, her deafness was transitory, but if she wanted to play that game…!) Mum sent off for the course with renewed hope, and settled down to work at the table behind her mother's chair, where the vibes were indirect.

She was much encouraged and fired off a series of stories and articles onto mainly deaf editorial ears. She showed them all, at first, to Dandan, who, having read them, or not, would respond, in the dead flat voice Mum remembered greeting her appearance in readiness for her first ball.

"Yes, dear, very nice."

Pathologically shy in her youth, Mum had longed for enthusiastic approval. Now, with mounting piles of rejection slips, her enthusiasm died. The coup de grace was delivered when she proffered, for approval, the scintillating article she had just completed, about Lightning Ridge, the opal mine to which Charles had flown her on her last visit to Australia. What a day they had! She had collected material for further research. The geology and history of the opals was riveting. They were beautiful! And it was wonderful to be up in the sky with her son.

"I don't think anyone would be interested in that."

Ironically, I received very similar responses from Mum to my poetry writing!

Mum called it a day, cancelled the rest of the course and forfeited the promised refund for failure, since she had not finished the course.

Her next effort towards occupation was to visit the doctor at the mental hospital. She had always felt, when visiting me that she was doing a good job in supplying me with a lifeline. Not many patients seemed to have visitors, and she might be able to perform this service for other people. The doctor passed her on to the administrator who suggested a variety of ways she might help. It did not include direct contact with the patients. Mum, always fearful of interfering, asked where she would be most useful and was sent to the geriatric ward. This was exactly what she was trying to escape from! She withdrew in embarrassment.

Meanwhile, I was in my element with my own premises again. I made new friends and renewed old ones, working hard by day weaving and gardening and visiting households in Heyshott in the evenings. Being naturally gregarious, I did not entirely like living on my own. But I found the world of oriental rugs absorbing and acquired skills, which would last me twenty-five years.

Alex was living a full life working twelve-hour nights and sleeping most of the day one week, then off up north the next to work on his farmhouse. For Dandan, the old order had gone. Previously, he had had time to take her out in his newest vehicle or play her favourite game, Bezique, ensuring she won. When he slept her friends would call. Life had suited them both perfectly. Now, her friends, thinking she was being looked after, called less often. Mum felt that it was not possible to make friends with Dandan's friends because she commanded total allegiance within her orbit. If Mum were to voice *her* opinion she would be disloyal to Dandan and appear churlish.

She sought desperately for alternative accommodation and built endless castles in the air. Already in debt to the Trustees' Bank on account of the extensions at John Peel's cottage, she could not realistically think of buying anything. In the unlikely event of finding a buyer, in its present incomplete state, she could only hope to obtain half its potential value; and comparative values in this part of the world were double those of the northern properties, so the most she could hope for was a tiny slit of a house on the street in town.

There was a most attractive old-world, semi-detached cottage, not two minutes' walk from the bungalow. Mum had been in it years before when the owner, an eccentric old lady who farmed a few isolated acres on top of the downs, had offered it to Simon, when his farming days came to an end, along with his marriage. Her health was beginning to fail; she was a lonely woman who loved only her farm, and saw in him a man whom life had treated badly as it had treated herself. He was glad to help her but had no understanding of her mind. His own need was to restore his self-respect, after the humiliation of divorce. He had been reared on a farm, farming was in his blood, and he and his wife had been on their own farm. Therefore it could be assumed that he was competent to run these few acres without interference; certainly not female interference! The old lady wanted to reassure herself that her beloved flock was in safe hands. He wished to be left to get on with the job.

He became more and more irritated by her concern, and began to show marked signs of the family imbalance, to such a degree that Mum persuaded him to call it a day. The doctor prescribed Valium.

The cottage now appeared to be for sale only, not to let. Another false hope was a tumbledown shack deep in the forest. Mum found it on a perfect spring day, surrounded by primroses with a pathway to the stream. The sun was shining, the birds singing of heaven; buds bursting in the coppice; rabbits unafraid. Her heart was high once more. If she could find out who owned it, it might be possible to buy this, at a price she could afford. She spent the next few days investigating. They were happy days, but when, at last, she located an owner, he was unwilling to sell.

Then she heard of a really suitable house for sale, which would be big enough for them all. It was in the same village, so accessible to all Dandan's friends. It had a large attic, which would accommodate Alex with a studio, with the coveted northern light, and a bedroom. There were adequate rooms for Dandan, Mum and me. There was plenty of garage space and a spacious garden, with a suntrap for Dandan and scope for both Mum and me to work. What could be more ideal? Surely our problems were over?

Mum, of course, could not buy it. But Dandan was living at the expense of Grandpapa's estate. Mum had never approached them for anything for herself, but when her brother's family had done so, the trustees had helped. Anyway, this was going to be for Dandan's benefit as much as her own. The trustees wrote saying that all the beneficiaries must be consulted. Some of the beneficiaries saw sinister undertones, and would take no chances in case a part of the estate was irretrievably bound up in the house after Dandan's departure, to Mum's benefit.

Mum was astonished and cut to the quick to receive the trustees' reluctant refusal, and their explanation. There was a heat wave at the time. One morning Mum woke up with a searing pain in her right arm. A draught perhaps? Whatever it was, the only relief she could find, was the application of a very hot water bottle, a series of them. Dandan nearly always hugged a hot water bottle, but didn't want one in this heat. Mum rather hoped that her agony would be noticed and a little sympathy forthcoming. There was none. The pain extended to her fingers, which she could no longer move. She went to the doctor.

The doctor sent her to an osteopath next door. Mum introduced herself: "I'm looking for someone to wring my neck," she repeated to him.

He was not amused.

"I'm afraid that wouldn't help," he said solemnly.

After examining her closely, he gave his verdict.

"There is some irreparable damage," he said, "but I can give you a massage which will relieve the pain."

Mum discovered, for the first time, the luxury of a professional massage.

"You should come back regularly for two or three months and we'll see how it goes."

Mum was appalled, imagining that she had somehow trapped a nerve and that all would be well after a manipulation.

"Thanks very much. That's much more comfortable, but I don't think I'll be coming again." Where was that sort of money coming from? She'd never been a private patient before. She knew, of course, what was really the matter, whatever he might say about irreparable damage. She needed a break. She had not had so much as a half-day off since she got back from Australia, eighteen months earlier. No. That was not true. A kind neighbour had taken Dandan off to watch Wimbledon with her, but Dandan had twigged that the kindness had been for Mum's benefit, rather than her own, and refused to go again.

In answer to her cry for help, I moved back in while Mum went back to John Peel's cottage. She had left an agency to let it in her absence but the agent found it impossible to keep in a satisfactory condition, with no one willing to undertake the cleaning. Mary from across the road had done her best, but had her own work to do, and when there was trouble with the drains from the farmyard at the back, and silt lay on the old restaurant floor, she kindly shovelled the carpet out onto the forecourt. But that was it. Unsuitable for visitors.

Mum had heard something of this but could not understand how the flood had happened, nor could anyone explain. It was just part of the frustration of being here when she should have been there. She was tied by the heel and tried to ignore it all. At last, she could do something about it all. It was simple enough. When they built the extension, a soak away had been installed in the yard, with pipes leading from it, below the extension, to drain away on the other side. The farmer's pipes had been inadvertently smashed, so that the water sat in the yard and travelled no further than the house itself. The builder was busy now but if she could bring her mother up for a month in October, he would be free to do all the jobs that remained to be done.

Chapter 7

Trio at Ruthwaite

Mum returned after a week, happy in the knowledge that her property was viable once more. She had spent her time dusting and polishing, freshening up the linen, and redeeming the relapsed wilderness that had been the garden. The car park, which had held six cars, their own and visitors', was unrecognisable when she arrived but, failing to make much headway with a borrowed scythe, she had tackled it with a kitchen knife (now much reduced in size), and dug out the docks and thistles by the roots: all excellent therapy for the useless hand which protested unnoticed.

During the summer I had rehearsed weekly with the Bart's Choir in London and went with them with a view to singing Aida in the Pyramids. With the change of leadership from Sadat to Mubarak we performed instead: *Alexander's Feast* by Handel in the British Embassy. I brought the only two Egyptian guests, wearing galabeyas, to the concert. On my return to England I was short of sleep and growing unsettled. My affairs were getting out of hand and the added responsibility of looking after Dandan had not helped. My "castle" had been invaded by another tenant who was a bona fide craft student. This was an older woman accustomed to running her own show. I'd grown used to thinking of the cottage as my own. There was friction. Mum could see that the situation was fragile.

Mum called in her brother and sister-in-law for a conference. She and her brother had always been good friends; he had visited regularly and Mum had taken Dandan over to visit them. She told him about her shoulder and her mounting worries about her neglected property, which, far from paying for its self, was quietly rotting away, while she paid the bank for the privilege of a loan. True, she had eaten at Dandan's expense but had taken nothing else and was now severely out of pocket. He had been most sympathetic and agreed that she really had earned a holiday.

"I've asked you to come over because I am not sure now how we are going to manage. Sal has done very well on her own but she is in some difficulty at the moment."

"What do you mean?"

"Her behaviour is erratic. She may have to go back to hospital. She will almost certainly lose her digs, and there's no room here."

"We'll do anything we can to help, naturally. We could look for someone to come and live with Dandan."

"That's not the point! Dandan and I can look for someone, with a better chance of finding her, but she does not want a stranger in her house. It's been bad enough for her having us."

"Well, I suppose we could come ourselves. Of course, we should need Dandan's bedroom…"

There was no need for further conversation. Dandan had been present at the conference, there being nowhere in the bungalow where it could have been held without her. The thought of her bedroom being occupied, and herself, perhaps, in the box room, did not appeal to her. Nothing was resolved. The crisis might not be immanent.

Dandan's mind was made up on one point; otherwise there was no conclusion.

Uncle Bim capitulated, "Whatever happens, you must not take Dandan from here!"

"I'd rather hoped to take her up for a month in October? The builder says he could finish all the little jobs that need doing, if I were there to supervise. And she'd love the autumn colours."

"She's not fit to travel that distance! You can't take her. If you try it I shall stop you!"

"What a very odd attitude," Mum thought, "and how could he stop me?"

The meeting was over and she thought no more about it. Very soon, with my sleepless nights and wanderings in the night through the village making unexpected calls, I was back in hospital, and out too soon. The kind weavers had no alternative but to give me a week's notice to clear my things. The moment came for instant decision. The hospital would not re-admit me; the neighbours were beginning to complain of outrageous behaviour and Mum had nowhere to contain me. The only course of action she could see was to take me back to John Peel's cottage where I would be known and understood. The local doctor had once told me: "We have a first class medical back-up team here, but we like to keep our patients out of hospital."

Mum approached her mother, "Dandan, I have to do something about Sal. She can't stay here and she can't go back to hospital. I'll have to take her back to Ruthwaite. I'd always promised you that you could die in your own home and that I would look after you as long as you needed me, but there are plenty of people who could look after you, and no one can help Sally, so we must go. Bim and Stella have said that they'll come themselves to look after you, or they will find someone else to live in – you must have somebody. Or do you want to come and live with us?"

"Oh, I'll come with you!" said Dandan without a moment's hesitation.

Mum was somewhat taken aback, but touched by her mother's unexpected choice.

"Sal and I have to go now. The place isn't fit for you to live in at present, but we'll get it ready for you, and Alex will bring you up on Saturday. That will give you time to look around for the things you most want to have with you."

The journey presented enough problems without the added imponderables of a third passenger. As it was, Mum and I set off with light hearts. Mum found me highly entertaining; both of us glad to shake the dust off our feet. It was one of those times between breakdown and recovery

59

when I could accept Mum's concern for me without reservation, a time when we were real friends. It was, perhaps, a sort of mutual euphoria when each of us was prepared to listen to the other.

The journey passed quicker than any other. We lit a fire, boiled a kettle and relaxed on arrival. Next day we reported to Dr Bob.

We set about preparing for Dandan's coming. The uneven stone staircase, for all it was wide and shallow-stepped, would not be safe for her, especially at night, with steps separating the bathroom from all the bedrooms. She would have to have the sitting room with its two rather high, small windows, as her bed-sitter. There was an open fireplace. The little alcove could be made into a hanging cupboard with a curtain in front. It would not hold many clothes, but she did not need all that many. There was room for two comfortable chairs by the fire. Her bed would go in the corner behind a screen; and there was room for her chest of drawers, her dressing table, fireside table and what about a commode? Mary kindly lent them one, which had belonged to her own mother. There was also a bathroom across the passage from Dandan's room, so we felt well pleased with our preparations.

Saturday morning came. We were having breakfast.

"Good heavens!" Mum cried out suddenly.

"What's the matter?"

"I've clean forgotten to tell uncle Bim that we've gone and that Dandan is coming too! He'll be furious. He said I wasn't to take her!"

"Why on earth not? What's it got to do with him?"

"Well he is her son, as much as I am her daughter."

"But you've always looked after her."

"Yes, but I should have told him. Even if he didn't mind her coming, he'll want to see her before she goes. He might not get another chance. Perhaps if I ring now, I might just catch him in time to nip over before they start."

She rang her brother and explained that there had been no evil intent in her oversight. Apologising, she suggested that if he were to ring now he should catch them, but only just, before they left.

"At least," she smiled to herself, "that will have forestalled any recriminations."

Alex and Dandan arrived in splendid time and in very good shape. Dandan had always loved speed. She was delighted with her room, cosy with its live fire, a comfort she had not enjoyed for years. Mum told them of her oversight regarding uncle Bim and asked if he had succeeded in catching them.

"Oh," said Alex, "that's who it was! I heard the phone ringing as I was locking the door, and nearly went back. But I thought it might delay us and couldn't really spare the time."

Mum was sorry for poor old Bim. He was fond of Dandan and would miss her badly: he might never see her again. She should not have been so inconsiderate. She should have thought more about Dandan's welfare too. Her mind had been full of concern for me, and Dandan had, after all, made her own decision.

The next morning the Reverend Tucker called. Dandan was delighted. This place was not so benighted after all! People had already heard of her coming and had come to visit. But when she realised he had come to see me and pray for my health, and had looked in on her in passing, she took a dimmer view.

"I never like men with beards," she declared.

The postman presently brought her a letter from Stella, who appeared to be in a terrific state following Dandan's sudden flight. She and Bim had gone over at once, as soon as they heard the news. They had been horrified to find the back door unlocked and no sign of anybody. They had gone in to see if everything was all right, and had found that no care had been taken to put things away. They were afraid that, looking through the window, someone might be tempted by Dandan's treasures. So they had packed them all up and had taken them for safe keeping to their bank. They couldn't bear to think of Dandan's treasures being left to chance like that: they would look after everything for her. They were so distraught to think of her being taken away, without their knowledge even.

Dandan was predisposed, by the rector's visit, to make the most of this. She wrote back that it was the greatest comfort to her to know that they were looking after her things for her. It had been a great shock to her. She had had no idea Alex was going to kidnap her. With all her love, etc. Mum was given this letter to vet and was furious. She had a few words of her own to add in answer. She addressed them to her brother.

"It was unfortunate that the back door was not locked, but it was not your responsibility. Primarily it was mine, or, perhaps as tenant, it was Alex's. There was no need for you to go over at all, since you had already ascertained that there was no one there. But as you feel so strongly about her not leaving her bungalow, and about her not being properly looked after, and have made her believe that she was kidnapped, I can only think that you will be coming with all speed to remove her. I look forward to your coming."

Peace was made in due course, and by mail. The next letter Dandan wrote contained the message, "I like my new cottage."

Mum ground her teeth and muttered, "Typical! It's not *her* cottage," as she put it in its envelope, having been asked to check it first.

Alex had to go straight back after delivering Dandan. (What is more he had to go an extra twenty miles to get the key which had been removed in his absence, before going on night duty.) None of them felt up to going to church so soon after Dandan's great journey, but the next Sunday, Mum felt that she should take her mother to church. Dandan had not been going lately, except to a small chapel for weekday services, which she could hear. Mum had not attended for years, but as Dandan was a staunch Christian, it might make her feel more at home and less confined by the four walls of her new prison.

They arrived at the lychgate with barely time to walk, at Dandan's speed, to the church. Mum had forgotten it was such a long path. Their progress was not helped by the fact that Dandan had donned a pair of bloomers whose elastic was not up to the job. Mum's embarrassment became ever more acute as she tried to race the last minute bell to the door. They just made it. I was waiting for them impatiently. Mum would have slunk into the nearest pew. But not Dandan. She insisted in leading her retinue, bloomers and all, right up to the front, and sat herself down beneath the pulpit. There was that man again, with the beard. She looked him unforgivingly in the eye throughout the service, and at the end announced: "The acoustics of that church are very bad. I couldn't hear a thing. I never like men with beards."

Evidently, it was no good going there again with Dandan.

I fell once more into the role of cook. Mum started the day as chambermaid, taking tea to her mother and preparing her bathroom, while she drank it. She turned on the electric heater and ran the hot water, knowing that Dandan would not run it long enough and would feel (if not complain) that there was no hot water. Then, while Dandan was in the bathroom, Mum would re-lay and light her fire so that it was warm enough to dress by. Meanwhile, I re-lit the Rayburn in the small dining room, which was also Mum's and my sitting room. Everything was geared towards Dandan's appearance at breakfast. It was not a very cheerful meal as a rule. We sat under the high window from which could only be seen a neighbour's chimney and a wide expanse of eternally grey sky.

"It's very grey today," was Dandan's invariable comment.

Grey sloth set the tone for the day but after breakfast there would be a slight rush for the sink. Clearing breakfast was a combined operation. We each of us had our own method, which was slightly different to the others, so it always started in mild confusion; but the main objective was the sink. Dandan liked to get there first and take charge of the washing up. She practiced the utmost economy.

"That doesn't need washing," she would say firmly, after peering closely at a knife or plate, still covered with marmalade. The things, which were not exempted, were swilled vaguely and handed to the drier. Once Dandan had established herself there was no ousting her. She was slightly handicapped by her walking speed, but, with the aid of her stick, she was well able to fill the passage, if not prevented. It was a matter of timing. One of the losers of the sink race would dry up, while the other would put away and boil the kettle for Dandan's hot water bottle. This was another job of which Dandan thought she was perfectly capable. Mum was not so sure and didn't want to find out.

After that, Dandan would take a duster and *do* her room. For this Mum was really grateful. Dandan had a great mass of memorabilia, photographs of five generations, pictures and ornaments. With an open fire, all these were inevitably thick with dust every day. It was a job that Dandan quite enjoyed but Mum would have found an intolerable waste of time. In a busy life, she had always justified her laziness with, "Dust will always wait till I am ready to deal with it," and it always did.

Mum worried that Dandan might be bored. Back at the bungalow she had sat all day, watching the blue sky and clouds contentedly, except when taken out in the car. Here the high window was hopelessly inadequate, and the clouds always grey. She suggested that she might like to play Patience, as her father had done.

"Yes, I should like that very much," Dandan brightened up as she took the cards out of their case. Mum brought a small table.

"Are you going to bring that chair for yourself?" Dandan asked.

"No, I thought you were going to play Patience?"

"Oh no! I don't want to play Patience. I thought you were going to play with me?"

Mum sighed. "Sorry, Mother, I really can't spare the time now. We'll play Bezique after tea, if you like." Dandan loved Bezique, and always won. She used to play it all day long if she could get anyone to play it with her, as Mum did in the old days when she used to visit her. Somehow they'd not played when they lived together. But Dandan had not forgotten how to play, though now the three of them played Hearts or Slippery Ann, which she had played with her children before they left home. She still played a wily hand.

Tea-time was something of a ritual, symbolising, as it did, more salubrious days, when Dandan was *at home* to her friends, and the children were brought, freshly scrubbed and polished for their entertainment. It was still at four o'clock sharp, but there the simile ended. The children were by no means scrubbed, and the dainty table of delicate sandwiches and petit fours were replaced by coarser chunks of buttered bun and mugs of tea. But the principle was the same: it was Dandan's room and she was still presiding.

Breakfast, lunch and supper we all ate together in the dining room where the Rayburn was. There were two fireside chairs so we treated it as *our* sitting room and Mum was at pains to make it clear that it was our private room, to which Dandan was welcome for meals, and in the evening to watch television, or by invitation. Perhaps she should not have bothered. The very fact that Dandan knew it was sometimes out of bounds made her all the more determined to be there. Why should she need an invitation? Had she not always made us welcome in her house? There was no room in which we did not go. Welcome? Really? Well...?

Supper was at seven o'clock. After tea, and the ensuing game of cards, Mum would fill Dandan's hot bottle and make up the fire and retreat "for a bit of peace". We would enjoy each other's company: reading, letter writing,

65

knitting or whatever. At six o'clock the door would open, slowly, and gradually Dandan's head would emerge round it.

"Oh, isn't supper ready?"

"No, Dandan," patiently, "it's only six o'clock. Supper isn't till seven."

"Oh, then I'd better go back to my room. (Pause for invitation; none forthcoming.) I'll go to my room then." (Shades of Old Steptoe pathos. Granite hearts.)

Or, "My fire's gone out; I thought I'd come and sit in here."

Mum, her heart ever hardening, would get up quickly, before Dandan had a chance to settle, "I'll make your fire up for you," and taking her gently but firmly by the hand, guided her back to her own domain. As often as not there was still a good fire burning.

"We'll come and tell you when supper is ready," she promised.

Or, "Is that really the time?" and she would come quickly up to the clock. "It says it is only a quarter past six. My watch must be wrong." It always was but there was not much wrong with her internal one. She always knew when it was four o'clock, or half past ten, Dubonnet time.

Sometimes Mum would relent. How could she be so beastly to a little frail old woman, not far off her century? She must want company. How could she turn her mother away like that? She must be an unspeakable monster. Which was exactly what Dandan was counting on. It was really incredible how she'd got Mum to believe that she had to look after her mother in her old age. She would never have done the same for her mother, in fact, she'd often told Mum how Gran had arrived, when newly widowed, as if to stay, and how Aunt Mary had said to her, "Is it wise, do you think, to take her to live with you?" And how she answered, "Certainly not! She's only coming for a week, I can promise you." She supposed she was lucky to have Mum. Pity she was so dull!

Dr Bob looked in one morning, to make her acquaintance, and was immediately approved. It was a social call, and when taking his leave, Mum took him to the door and told him that she was afraid the old lady might miss all her friends, and her fascinating view and might feel bored.

He reassured her, "She looks remarkably well. She's settled in splendidly, hasn't she? You don't have to worry about her at all; you can get on with your own life! She'll be no trouble, I'm sure." Mum was less certain, but was comforted.

Chapter 8

Garlands

Peter Dalglish had moved to Lancashire in 1965, with his second wife, Betty, known to the family as Min. For the last two years he had been suffering from cancer of the pancreas and died in the spring, 1984, six months after we all moved to John Peel's cottage. Simon, who had a haulage business, had worked on the farm on and off for many years. Recently, he and Min had done everything, allowing the "old man" to think he was running it still. Now they expected to run it their own way, together.

Alex, alone now in his grandmother's bungalow was deeply shocked by his father's death, and suddenly felt very lonely. He packed in his job, helped the trustees to sell up, and dispose of Dandan's furniture and effects (such as were not already in his uncle's bank), according to his grandmother's Will. Now, at last, he must get back to Higher Clough in earnest.

Mum thought how wonderful it would be for all the family to join up, and when lambing was safely over, she suggested that they might meet for a picnic at a beauty spot halfway between them. Alex came with Simon and Min who were bursting with excitement over the prospect of a holiday. They were going to stay with Charles and his family in Australia. Min had never been before.

I immediately piped up: "Can I come too?"

No one had anticipated such a thing. I couldn't see any reason why I shouldn't. It would be a whole lot more fun than living at John Peel's cottage. The answer of course was: "No." Having to explain it cast a blight on the day. In any case, who was going to pay for my fare? How could everyone else afford these things when I never could? And there was the nasty thought that I might not be able to get a visa. (Actually, Australia seems to be more enlightened about manic-depressive illness than UK. But, at that time ignorance and stigma seemed to shroud the disease.)

Simon wondered if the John Peel contingent would like to take a self-catering holiday at Wicken Clough, in exchange for feeding the dogs and hens and seeing to the mail while they were away. Mum thought it a stunning idea. There was a breathtaking view out of Simon's living room window, one to equal Dandan's from her old bungalow. She would love it, and it would give them all a change of scene. And there would be Alex down the road.

I was less than euphoric. I could not forget that Simon and Min were going to Australia and not going to take me. My sleep patterns became erratic. My writing went off at a tangent in my current journal until I was writing torrents of stuff that meant nothing to anyone but me. I was talking too much and becoming imperious and uninhibited. It was not long before I was in hospital, a new one to me: Garlands. Dr Bob had tried to keep me out, till now. For Mum it was very disappointing. But she thought that if I had to have a breakdown this summer, it was best to get it over now, before it could interfere with the holiday plans. It usually took me ten days to a fortnight to come home again.

That's what Mum thought. But after three weeks I was still not ready to come out. Mum visited me every day, as always, taking Dandan along for the ride. At first one was taken to the reception block, as inviting as a private hospital, but I progressed to the locked ward, a room of intermittent shrieks and yells where those that smoked stubbed their fag ends on the floor and those that had no tobacco gathered the threads of tobacco from the butts and rolled thin cigarettes. Periodically someone would turn all the taps full on and leave them. The staff had to be quick to avert flooding. Inmates would come up to me and speak gibberish.

Sometimes Mum and I would walk in the grounds while Dandan stayed in the car. Or we might all three go for a cup of tea in the canteen and I would wander off to join other patients. One day we took the car further afield and went for a walk by the riverside. Our respective paces were incompatible along the track so Mum paced herself with Dandan while I walked ahead. I was well ahead before Mum realised that there was a place for hiring boats. I spotted a family about to board ship and joined them.

Mum remembered the occasion, when, taking her four infants to the seaside, she had been clutching the smallest, Alex, on the edge of an in-coming tide, when there were anguished yells from Charles and Simon who had found themselves in difficulties further out, in an unsuspected pool. If she had dropped Alex, no doubt he would have drowned, and if she didn't reach Charles and Simon in time, they might as easily have drowned too. I meanwhile was safely collecting shells. We all survived.

Now, faced with the same dilemma, Mum was tempted to jettison Dandan, but fortunately the hirers of the boat saw her consternation and diverted my attention. Such goings on persuaded Mum that I was not fit yet to emerge from hospital, and I seemed content to stay. As time went on Mum began to wonder if I'd be out in time for the holiday. At each visit I was pleased to come for a walk or a drive but showed no signs of being ready for home.

Finally, the day before we were due to take over Wicken Clough, they came and I appeared to be worse than ever. When walking with Mum in the grounds I suddenly spotted a fireman and his engine in the middle of an exercise. I ran off to talk to him and begged a ride on his engine. Before he knew it, I was up in his cab and refused to get out. I took no notice of Mum or anyone else. In the end Mum had to admit defeat and went to the office, where a cheerful administrator came to the rescue.

"Come on, love," he said

"Oh, there you are," I cried, putting my arms round him happily and trotting back with them to the ward.

It was not a very good start to the holiday. Mum didn't know what to do. She hated leaving me there, though she had told me earlier that she would have to if I were not ready for discharge. She could not let Simon and Min down. They had their tickets and couldn't change. And she certainly didn't want to think of letting me loose at John Peel's cottage in her absence. All she could do was to ask the hospital doctor to keep me in until she came back.

The doctor was reluctant but suggested that under the circumstances he might be able to keep me in on a twenty-eight-day section. Mum went away relieved to know that at least I would be safe. Sadly, she and Dandan set off without me. In the evening Simon showed Mum all the peculiarities of her various new charges. The phone was ringing as they came back into the house.

"It's for you, Mother," Simon said, handing her the phone.

"Is that Mrs Dalglish?"

"Yes."

"Mrs M. K. Dalglish?"

"Yes."

"This is the welfare officer at Garlands. Mrs Dalglish, what do you mean by abandoning your daughter in Garlands?"

He sounded as if he thought Mum was trying to get rid of me.

"I haven't abandoned her!" she said indignantly. "I would have brought her with me if she had been fit. I spoke to Dr Srinivassan about her."

"And do you propose to visit her while you are away?"

"Of course I do! I have always visited her. But I can't come every day from this distance – I'm a hundred miles away. Probably twice a week?"

"Your daughter called me in some distress this afternoon. I have been to see her, and I must say that I can see no reason why she should be held here. When will you be coming to see her?"

"I'll come tomorrow, if you feel like that."

"I'll meet you on the ward at half past eleven."

Alex had looked in to greet his mother and grandmother, and promised to look after things while Mum was away so, as soon as Simon and Min were on their way in the morning, Mum retraced her steps to Garlands.

There was no sign of the welfare officer, but I greeted Mum pleasantly, as if nothing in the world were the matter. I was all packed, looking immaculate, with a head as clear as that of a top executive. I explained that Dr Srinivassan had not signed anything yet, but was poised to sign by midday, if Mum still thought it necessary. In the meantime, I hoped that Mum would agree with the welfare officer and me, that it was not. Mum had to admit that if anyone were sane round her, it was I.

"You're a naughty little monkey!"

Dr Srinivassan suggested, wisely, that I should go out on a forty-eight hour pass. If all went well, he could sign me off over the phone; if not, I could return to the hospital. Once signed off I would be in a different catchment area and would have to start all over again, with a new medical team. *No, thank you,* Mum thought, *we'll stick to the lot we know, if we need anyone.*

I remained on my best behaviour – until safely signed off. Then I felt on top of the world. And why shouldn't they all suffer a little, having left me behind like that. I never would have believed it of Mum. They could always have cried off and left Alex to cope (which had never occurred to Mum). Feeling high, I did not feel that I needed to take my medication. Dr Srinivassan was a firm believer in lithium carbonate for hypomanics, but it needed to be taken continuously. Mum could not persuade me to take the pills.

Dandan, not to be outdone, said, "If Sally is not going to take her pills, I'm not going to take mine."

Dandan was supposed to take iron pills, but periodically went on strike. This was a good cue for mutiny.

Alex, seeing that Mum's charges were almost unmanageable, came every day to give his support. It was heroic of him, since he was already finding life hard going. He hated friction and violence, as much as Mum did. Mum, unable to bang the heads together of her two spoilt charges, wondered whether it would be best to separate them. Alex agreed to keep Dandan and tend to the livestock, while Mum and I retreated once more to John Peel's cottage on our own. Peace reigned in both camps.

Dandan returned triumphantly, in due course to announce: "That was a lovely holiday Alex and I had."

Chapter 9

Warwick Square

During the next few months I found it harder and harder to get and keep a job. Pricking out seedlings at a local nursery became too tedious. I applied to a Jewish organic café in Keswick.

"What are your qualifications?"

"Ten O-levels, four A-levels, an honours degree and a post graduate."

"Why are you applying for this post as a waitress?"

"To learn humility."

"Pah!" he looked at me warily. "YOU will never have humility!"

But still he took me on, and later fired me for "attitude" with the customers. Waitressing in a busy tourist town was very different from running my own show, in my own time. It was depressing, and the atmosphere at home was far from cheering.

One day Mum spotted an advert in a local paper: "New members welcomed by group studying Gurdjieff."

This was presumably similar to a group John and I had been with in Yorkshire. Dr Kenneth Walker, a friend of my father's in Heyshott had worked with Gurdjieff at Fontainebleau. I was not as committed as John had been, but it seemed that this might be the opening that I was looking for. I applied, joined and attended weekly meetings in Carlisle. In Yorkshire, we spent whole weekends actively observing our "thinking", "moving" and "emotional" centres. In Abbey Street, we were just lectured to.

"What on earth are you doing, hiding yourself away with those two old women?" a couple of the group asked me. "You should be living your own life, doing something worthwhile."

"There are reasons," I was chary about being too specific. For many people the mention of mental illness rang alarm bells. In the age of ignorance: fear, stigma and contempt were too often awakened. But these people were not alarmed, only dismayed to think of a talented young woman wasting her life.

"Rubbish!" they said. "We'll find you a bedsitter. Come and live near us. We'll look after you." Catherine, who made the offer, I have now known for thirty years.

This was tremendously exciting for me and Mum was delighted. I had come to a dead end and this looked like a door into a new world. My new friends and I found an upstairs room at the back of an old Victorian house, now let off as rooms and flats. My promise to look after the garden reduced the rent satisfactorily. Very soon, taking my precious Persian rugs and enough furniture, I installed myself in my new home and took up gardening for residents at Scotby and coaching, mostly nine-year olds trying to gain a place at Austin Friars. I would try and home in on a pupil's main interest and spent a lot of time studying woodlice with one enthusiast.

In the house there was a vast Victorian kitchen available to all residents, but some had their own kitchenettes and were young and single, and mostly out. The kitchen was important to me so I had no difficulty in making it largely my own and was even given permission to redecorate it. What with the refurbished kitchen, the newly loved garden and the overflow of Persian rugs, I could be seen to have added tone to the place. It was gratifying to be offered, when it became vacant, the lower front room, the drawing room of better days – at the same affordable rent.

Rugs concealed my bed and mundane apparatus of living. At Catherine's suggestion I drew on my savings and bought a baby grand piano. "It's good for the emotions." She and her husband regularly invited me to

75

Chatsworth Square for a meal, beautifully prepared. Members of the group called on me and might almost have got the impression that I was chatelaine of this whole, huge mansion and garden. Dandan approved: it was a suitable setting for her granddaughter. Why couldn't Mum have found somewhere like this to live instead of her scruffy little cottage?

Not that Dandan ever complained. She was even grateful, sometimes, for her fire, and loved going out for drives. She appreciated the beauty of the countryside, and indeed, when they were driving or sitting side by side in the car, rather than opposite one another, they seemed to be able to talk on level terms, as friends. But the moment they were back in the house, they were at war, undeclared but unmistakable.

It had always been fun getting a rise out of Mum, Dandan reflected. She was so dull, so, good – so utterly boring. She remembered the time when Cousin May was dying and she'd thought of sending Mum over to spend the night with her. Mum was working two or three nights a week, but had a daytime job as well. She looked in, as usual, after a long day.

"Oh, Moll, I rang Cousin May today. She's in a very bad way I'm afraid. I said I'd go and look after her tonight. She doesn't seem to have anybody."

"Don't you think that, at eighty-six, it might be a bit much for you?"

"Well, I'm beginning to wish I hadn't!"

"Do you think I ought to offer?"

"Would you, Moll?" with the air of a penitent old Silly Billy.

"I suppose so. You do get yourself into some holes, don't you?"

Who but a fool would have fallen for such a thing? Mum found a surprised and competent housekeeper in charge, and one or two lookers-on. Cousin May allowed her to cut her toenails, by way of compensation.

One night at Ruthwaite, two chairs had been left inadvertently in the passage between Dandan's bed-sitting room and her bathroom. Mum had always insisted on her putting the light on but Dandan had always insisted on economy. She didn't need a light. She knew her way perfectly well. Tripping over the obstacle in the passage Dandan fell and cut her shin. It did not hurt, but it bled a lot.

The doctor came. When he applied the anesthetic needle to her almost fleshless leg she said with forbearance: "Young man, you're hurting!"

He stitched the skin down her shinbone with consummate skill. A whole series of nurses came to do the dressing each day, and one or other of the doctors would pop in from time to time to see how she was getting on. This was more like it. It was quite a bad gash and as is the way of old flesh, it took several weeks to heal. But at last it did heal and life became insufferably dull once more.

She was obviously in pain one morning, as she lost the race to the sink. Mum was concerned.

"What's the matter, Mother? You seem to be in pain."

Dandan had had the hip operation done some years ago (and recovered in double quick time), but Mum had been warned that it might not last. Now Dandan put her hand to her hip and flinched.

"I think it's my hip. I don't feel I can depend on it. It gives way, like that," she staggered.

It was Friday and it was snowing. Sometimes it was difficult to get along their lane in bad weather. Mum calculated that the doctor would not want to come on a Saturday, especially if the roads were worse and he might be out this way anyway today. Better give him the option, in case. He came, cheerfully, and after a little chat, asked, "And how do you walk, Mrs Longridge?"

She brightened. "Like anybody else, I suppose."

"Let's see you."

Dandan shot out of her chair, walked smartly to the door, and was through it, along the passage and up the steps to the dining room before anyone noticed that she had forgotten her stick.

"I'm sorry to have brought you out unnecessarily," Mum laughed as she showed the doctor out.

"Don't worry! It's always a pleasure to come out and see her. She's marvellous, isn't she?"

And indeed Mum was assured by the receptionist at the surgery that the doctors used to vie with each other for the privilege of visiting her.

One of them, Dr O'Brien, may have wished that he had not been the lucky one. He arrived when she had just settled down for a nap, after her morning glass of Dubonnet. This would not have mattered but he had come to give her an iron injection. This was a long fought battle, which Dandan was under the impression she had won. She had in no uncertain terms made it quite clear that she was not having them. Dr O'Brien had passed Mum at work in the garden as he came in and assured her he didn't need her in attendance. He emerged presently looking rather sheepish.

"Your mother is looking very well, isn't she? I thought perhaps she didn't need her injection this week."

At lunch Dandan, rage still smouldering in her eyes, demanded: "Who was that horrid little man with the red beard, who came to see me this morning?"

Poor Dr O'Brien was quite a big man, and clean-shaven. But, in her eyes, any man who proposed to inject her against her will was horrid, and automatically bearded. If he was at the bottom of her social list, his beard was necessarily red. In case he should read this and feel hurt, she did say, after another less threatening visit, "Who was that charming man?"

Chapter 10

Bloodbath

I was safely launched in my new life and had acquired a number of new guardian angels. Dandan was contained at John Peel's cottage and Mum began to yearn for another visit to Australia. She had worked hard until retirement to enable her to keep in touch with them every two years or so, and, in spite of everything, was not far behind schedule.

Alex had come to her rescue at Wicken Clough and it was to him she turned to now. He would come and look after Dandan while she was away. They were such good friends. They would enjoy it.

But it wasn't like that. He arrived two days sooner than he was expected, but Mum, delighted to see him, thought nothing of it. She came back from Australia to find that it had not been a very happy visit. Dandan had been rebellious and made a scene with one of the nurses who visited her, and she had led Alex – her beloved Alex – a fearful dance. He was convinced that she harboured a grudge against his abducting her, and would never forgive him. He was distressed but lingered on, unexpectedly, after Mum's return. He seemed reluctant to go home. Admittedly "home" was his unfinished farmhouse, which he had been restoring with a shilling for ten years. It was damp and uncomfortable, and winter was coming.

What was worse, his friends seemed to have melted away and he was not on good terms with Simon and Min. He was labouring with the roof and plastering; probably only feeding himself on baked beans on toast, and he was utterly alone. Mum tried to persuade him to stay with them but he refused and eventually went. She was worried about him. When she and Dandan had gone to see him each month during the summer, he had always talked nineteen to the dozen: lots of people living alone do. He had had a lot on his mind, and he had not got over his father's death. Loneliness was not good for anyone. She was worried, but she was not scared stiff, as she should have been. Even when he rang one evening in great excitement, telling her that he had given up being an artist and was now a writer! He had written a thrilling thesis, which was going to solve all the problems of the world. Even then she was not unduly alarmed. She should have remembered the copious journals I had written, which more than one psychiatrist was interested in.

It was not until next morning, when Simon phoned to say that Alex had just phoned to ask him to pick him up and take him home with him: "Mum, can you come down?"

It was then that fear really gripped her. She bundled Dandan into the car and sped down to Wicken Clough. The two men were in the kitchen, equally troubled. Alex was talking poppycock; Simon close to tears. They sat Dandan in a chair facing the view, where she was happily self-absorbed, while they tried to decide what to do.

The root of the trouble was their father's Will. He had told his family what to expect. It had not been possible to make it fair, but he had done his best, and everybody understood and accepted, without greed or envy. But when the Will was read, it bore no resemblance to expectation, and everyone was hopping mad. The lawyers were having a field day. Mum, after her divorce, had vowed that she would never employ a lawyer again as long as she lived (and consequently she had to do her own conveyancing), so she knew how they felt.

At the moment, the problem was: what to do next? Simon lived on his own at Wicken Clough, a barn he had bought from his father, and converted into a most attractive home, while Min lived on in the farmhouse. Mum was tempted now to pick up both boys and take them to John Peel's cottage where she could look after them.

But Simon said, "I'll have to stay to look after the livestock. Min's away."

Mum remembered his girlfriend, who had looked in while he was away. She would look after him, gladly. Simon, too, had had trouble before, and knew when to take Valium. He would be all right.

Alex needed a doctor. The only one they could trust was back in Cumbria. An added complication was Alex's newly acquired dog. A passing neighbour had been concerned for his loneliness and found a dog for him that might otherwise have been shot, as a work-shy collie. She was a bitch and Alex fell for her at once, seeing in her the perfect companion. By the time Mum arrived he was wholly absorbed in Jess. His thinking was very muddled and he was trying to work out the relationship between DOG and GOD: they were interchangeable.

Getting her into the car was an exercise of supreme patience. The poor little beast had come fresh from the farm, one of a litter, but fully grown. She was not accustomed to cars or people. To Mum's relief, Alex agreed to sit in the back with the dog and she was allowed to drive. It would have been nice to get Dandan packed in first, but the car had only two doors, so she had to wait till Jess could be persuaded to jump in. Alex was determined that she must *want* to come with him. God must not be coerced.

At last they were all in, Simon having waved them goodbye. He had told Mum that when he had collected Alex that morning he had found him ready with everything packed up and put away, as if for a long absence. He brought a suitcase with him now.

So, it had happened: the thing that had been staring them in the face for a year or more. Yet we hadn't believed it could really happen. We knew he was vulnerable. I had broken, carrying the same genes. Simon had nearly broken on several occasions, and Alex himself had narrowly escaped on more than one occasion. How could we have been so confident that he was unbreakable? How could we have allowed him to live alone and not seen how distraught he was? Was it not obvious what would happen? With shock and guilt Mum thought of Alex labouring in that dismal remote farmhouse when he had been accustomed to being surrounded by the young bustling staff at The Sanatorium.

"We are all so bound up in our own little worlds," she reflected, "and all wearing blinkers. But what could we have done, anyway? Is there a force, which decrees such things or do we really have a say in the matter?"

Alex's first thought on arrival at Ruthwaite was to take his thesis to show Les, who lived in Caldbeck some six miles away. I had met him at one of Catherine's parties at Chatsworth Square. As they watched me chopping pistachio nuts, with gusto, with a huge Sabatier kitchen knife, Les raised an eyebrow, "Psychotic?"

Now that I lived in Carlisle, I came out to John Peel's cottage every weekend and visited Les on the way back. He would give me an hour's therapy analysing my dreams and the paintings I did every week, being a retired psychotherapist. Alex had met him when staying with Dandan. They were both artists, but when the conversation turned to me, Les commended my brilliance and excellence, and Mum suspected that the therapist in him was trying to impress them with something that they had missed.

"He doesn't know the summat!" Alex had laughed when they came out. It was a reference to the Cheshire farmer who had bought a horse at auction, and located the previous owner.

"Now I've paid thee, what's the summat?"

"What do you mean?"

"What do you mean?"

"Well there's always summat wrong, isn't there?"

With me, the "summat" was my unfortunate capacity for lacerating my nearest and dearest, when under the weather.

Now Alex was anxious to return to Les and show him his thesis, which was the most important thing in the world.

"Couldn't you leave it till the morning?" Mum asked. He seemed to be fairly settled after the journey and it was a pity to risk being churned up again.

"I must take it now. I want him to read it. It's very important."

"Well, if you must. But why don't you just take it over now and leave it with him to read?"

"All right, I won't be long."

He rang to warn Les of his coming. As soon as he was out of the house, Mum phoned Les to ask him to send Alex straight back. As it happened, Les had already rung me to ask me to come over and invited his daughter, who was a nutritionist. Unkempt, Alex arrived in a long beige duffle coat tied with bailer twine. His limbs and hands were stiff. Wendy could see he was in need of potassium and we tried to coax him to drink hot chocolate and eat a banana but he kept making triangles with his hands and refusing to put the banana in his mouth. Alex only wanted to discuss his thesis with Les. It was too private to be discussed in public. He felt himself outnumbered. He was uncertain of himself. He didn't know what was going on. He felt himself to be sinking into a horrible black pit, the void. He may have blacked out momentarily.

Wendy, who also taught the Alexander Technique tried to help him relax as he lay on the floor. He began to see Les as a devil and Wendy and me as witches. I was the last person he would have wanted to see at this moment, for he was a proud man. He had always been the one to support me, and therefore, although he was younger, he had always felt like an elder brother. How are the mighty fallen? His defeat could hardly be more bitter.

We managed to calm him down enough to return home; if he was still disturbed, at least he didn't wander. Perhaps even he slept. Next morning Mum announced her intention of sending for the doctor. Alex made a point of being out,

83

walking his dog, when he saw the man coming. Mum apologised. Alex spent the day quietly, walking with Jess, or sitting by the fire, which Mum had lit in the old restaurant. He seemed content, but quiet. Sometimes Mum sat with him. He told her of the visit last night. Sometimes he seemed to want to be left alone to think things out. In the evening she took him his supper on a tray and returned to do her stint with Dandan. (Why was Alex getting all the attention?)

When she returned the fire was out. He'd said not to make it up. The French window was wide open, and the room an icebox. She went into the yard and called. No answer. He didn't have a coat. He'd be perished. There was ice on the puddles and the grass was all frosty. She saw the moon overhead, much larger than the moon should be. Malevolent. How can a moon look malevolent? It did, that's all. It was Halloween.

Mum shivered and went in. The first thing was to pack Dandan off to bed; then she could think what to do. At last she put on her coat and boots and wandered about calling his name. Suddenly, she thought, *My God! He'll have gone to see Les! And what sort of mood will he be in? He may well think he has some unfinished business there.* A young man in his prime, with manic tendencies and a grudge, might not be the most welcome visitor. Perhaps he was there already? Mum rushed off in the car, and seeing a telephone kiosk, stopped and rang Les.

"No. He's not here."

"Thank heavens for that!" Mum said. "But where on earth can he be?"

Speculation was fruitless, and Les agreed that the police must be called. She rang them from the same box.

"Where are you calling from?"

Mum told them.

"If you look out of the door, you should see our lads across the road."

Sure enough, there was a police car, which she had not noticed. She tapped on the window. The policeman asked her to wait in her car until they had finished their business. Presently, one came out and escorted her back to John Peel's cottage, where he asked her about Alex. While she tried to revive the embers of Alex's old fire, he noticed the "Rembrandt" self-portrait with Alex's signature on it.

"That's a masterpiece, isn't it?"

"It's a copy of one." Mum was bursting with pride. "Not bad, is it?"

"It's good. Very good. Did your son do that?"

They spoke of the tragedy that accompanies such talent.

"Do you think your son would take his own life?"

"No. I don't think so. Anyway, how could he? He has no gun and no poison. And there's no knife sharp enough in this house."

"What about the river?"

That was a chink in the armour. She hadn't thought of that. But it was a long way from a river. Surely that little stream down the road could hardly be thought of as a river? Yet that was the one he was thinking of.

"Has he ever been violent?"

"What? Alex?" Mum laughed. "He's the gentlest man on earth! He even drapes a towel in the bath to let the spiders walk free."

"Is your daughter ever violent?"

"No, never," she said at once. But that was more difficult. My tongue was violent at times, but she'd never seen me hit anyone. Then she recalled the six men holding me down for an injection and hastily added, "Only when she's provoked, and that's fair enough, surely?"

It seemed that the call, which brought the police out, was from a young woman, near the phone box, who had gone out to get more firewood. She had surprised someone walking through the garden. He had run off when she jumped in fright. No mention of a dog. Could it have been Alex?

The other officer arrived and together the three of them patrolled the lanes, covering a wide area where Alex might be. No luck. In the end they took Mum back to the cottage and asked to use the phone. That was in the sitting room, now Dandan's. There was nothing for it but to show the man where it was. Dandan, mercifully, was well under the influence. How indignant she would have been to find a policeman in her room!

The officers departed saying that they would be in touch if there were any news. After another hour, one returned to say that they had sighted Alex a mile away and had spoken to him. They had offered him a lift, but he had declined. Wisely, perhaps, remembering Mum's postscript about me, they had not insisted. This officer led Mum to the spot where Alex had been seen, but he was no longer in sight.

"He said he was looking for his dog," the other man said. "He went that way, across the field. He said to tell you not to worry, he'd be back for breakfast."

That was a colossal relief to Mum. He was all right then.

"That's fine then! If he says he'll be back, I'm sure he will be. So there's no need for you to bother any more. Thank you both very much for all your help. We'll be all right now – and if we're not, I'll give you another ring. Goodnight."

It will be easier to find him now they've gone, she thought, and followed the lane in the direction indicated. The road looped round in a large circle, with Ruthwaite forming a tangent. He must be somewhere in that loop. He must have been able to hear her call in the still night air. She might even see him in the moonlight. There was no answer to her calls and no movement that she could see, though she stopped every now and again. For another hour or so she sought him, then, comforting herself with his promise, she went home.

The light was on. She must have left it on in her rush to find him, when the policeman came for her. She went into the kitchen and wrote a note for him, lest he come in before she came down in the morning.

"What a long walk! See you at breakfast time. Love, Mum." Just to let him know she loved him still, and that nothing else mattered. Sadly, she went upstairs. Her room was to the left at the top of the stairs. Something made her turn right and open his door. The room was dark and silent. But what was that smell? With realisation, the smell intensified – the unbelievably beautiful smell of wet dog! She almost cried for joy, but kept quiet, fearing to wake him. She crept away to her own bed, ready to sleep.

Presently, she was roused by the sound of a heavy, stumbling tread in the passage, shambling unsteadily into the bathroom. At the same time there was a prolonged groaning, a terrible, unearthly sound, such as she had never heard. Mum was paralysed with fear. What could be the matter? For a moment she froze then pulled herself together. She put on her dressing gown and opened the door. The passage was covered with a trail of bloody footprints, both right and left. Right up to the bathroom door. The door was shut. The light was showing under it. The bath water was running. Then it stopped. She called, "Alex?"

No answer.

"Alex, can I come in?"

"No."

"Won't you want some dressings for your feet?"

"I suppose so," faintly.

"I'll see what I can find."

Mum had never kept a first aid box, relying only on a packet of Band Aid plasters and a bottle of TCP for instant succour. These were clearly inadequate for this emergency. She thought of cutting up a sheet. Not very sterile, with her brand of home laundry. I know! There's that old packet of lint, left over from nursery days, when they sold the stuff by the pound. Out of fashion even in her St. Thomas's training days, and terrible stuff for sticking, but she could soak it off at leisure when things had settled down. That chap in the war had always asked for her to do his dressings. Perhaps it would not hurt all that much, and anyway, it was all she had.

This time she was allowed in. There was no lock on the door. If it was shut, there was someone in, no need for a lock. He lay in the bath, the water discoloured with blood. She sat on a stool.

"Somebody pulled the plug on me," he said coyly.

"What do you mean?"

"Somebody told the police. They were after me."

"I had to ring them, darling. You were out so late, and I didn't know where you were. Where did you get to?"

"I wandered up to Ireby, then went on through the churchyard. It was horrible. There were a lot of spirits there: evil spirits. I didn't stay there long, I can tell you." He was speaking very quietly.

"Where did you go next?"

I took Jess down to the bridge and made her sit there."

"Why did you do that?"

"I wanted to make sure she'd stay sitting, like Dad's dogs used to."

Mum's heart felt chilled: the bridge? The river? The waiting dog?

"What then?"

"I left her there and went on up to Uldale. There was no one around, so I walked through some of the gardens."

"Then I rang the police. They'd already come out because someone was frightened by seeing somebody in their garden."

"That wasn't me. I didn't see anybody."

"What happened to your feet?"

"I lost my shoes. I was running so hard that they were left behind in a bog. I remember those gardens and walking in them, but it couldn't have been me."

Mum could hardly bring herself to look at his feet. He spoke again, in a voice she could hardly hear.

"I think a man should be allowed to end it all when he's had more than he can take."

"You mustn't think like that, my darling." Tears welled up in Mum's eyes. "No one has more to bear than he can; you can always take a bit more than you think! And what would I do, if you were to give up?"

"All right. I won't do it."

"Promise?"

"Promise – just for you."

Mum left him, as he asked, with the pound of lint, two crepe bandages, safety pins and a pair of scissors, to wallow a little longer in his bath.

Chapter 11

Christmas at Wicken Clough

The police rang at nine o'clock, before she had done his dressing.

"Yes. He came back soon after you left me. He's perfectly all right, only he's hurt his feet. Thanks very much for ringing."

"I'm afraid we shall have to come and see him."

"No, there's no need for that, really. I'm hoping he'll sleep now. I can tell you anything you want to know."

"You misunderstand me. We have to take a statement."

"Oh, I see."

More red tape! She could have done without this. The house was filthy. She'd been busy in the garden, and the dust was still waiting for her; it hadn't shown in artificial light, or at any rate she hadn't noticed it. But the sun was shining now and that always let her down. And there was Alex's dressing to do. She couldn't hurry over that, or it would be agony for him. Better leave that till after they had gone. They wouldn't take long. She must try and make the house look as if she kept it clean.

Her shame had dwindled by the time they came, and she showed them up to Alex's room. Jess was peeping anxiously from under the bed and Alex greeted them politely. They asked him about his whereabouts last night and he told them, without embarrassment.

"We received a complaint from a woman who surprised a stranger in her garden shed."

"It wasn't me," quite calmly. "I remember walking through some gardens, but I never saw anyone."

"What happened to your feet?"

Had they seen the bloody footprints? They could hardly have missed them. She'd forgotten all about them.

"My shoes came off and I left them behind."

"Can I see them, please?"

Mum dreaded what was to come.

"I haven't dressed them yet."

"Never mind that."

No, but it is going to hurt like hell if the dressing is pulled off! Actually, they came off unhurriedly, without appearing to hurt unduly. The pain didn't seem to have bothered him too much since that awful trek down the passage. And there they were, those feet that she had dreaded seeing. Raw, with some bones showing through. And he had refused painkillers.

"Have you sent for the doctor?"

"No. I was going to dress them myself, after you'd gone."

"I'll give him a ring. Thank you, sir," he turned to Alex.

She took them down to the telephone. Another intrusion. Dandan was oblivious, sitting by the fire in her chair. Then she took them through to the restaurant where they sat down to await the doctor. The inspector looked accusingly at Mum.

"Those feet are in a dreadful state."

"I know," said Mum, ashamed. No good as a housewife, and no good as a nurse. How could any nurse, let alone one with her training, not take proper care of feet like that? Her own son's feet. She couldn't even claim to be a good mother when it came to requesting her harp.

"We'll have to go to Garlands."

"Oh no. He'll be all right now. We've been talking things over and he'll be all right. I can look after him."

Did she see a raised eyebrow?

"He must be manic. No one in his right mind could have such self-inflicted wounds."

Mum was not persuaded. He might have been manic, that was beside the point.

"We can insist," he said, gently.

That was it then.

"I must tell him."

Alex was waiting for her. Did he know already? She kneeled by the bed. A cold nose and a wet tongue greeted her hand as she pulled her skirt away. She put her arm around Alex's chest and her cheek against his and spoke softly in his ear.

"Dr Bob is coming out to do your dressing properly. The policemen want you to go to hospital, but it isn't for long."

"Do I have to go?"

"Sorry, darling, but I'm afraid you do. They may want you to have an injection. I know you hate that; but it is better to take it."

Dr Bob made a simple professional job of the feet, and Alex said, unprompted, "I'll take the injection." And very soon they were bowling along in the ambulance. Mary, from across the road, kindly came over to give Dandan her lunch.

Like me, he was taken to the five-star end of the hospital. Unlike me, he was on his best behaviour, his very best. He told the doctor that he didn't take medicine; he didn't believe in it. Could he please be allowed to get better in his own way?

"All right. We'll give it a try. But if you can't do it your way, you must let me try mine, OK?"

"Fine, thanks."

Alex could not claim to be feeling perfectly normal. He was still full of concern for the real meaning of life. His thesis was still with him, in his mind, and he was still conscious of the magnitude of creation and his own part in it. He did not actually see God or hear Him. But he was very much aware of Him.

He enjoyed visitors, but begged Simon, "Don't make me laugh! They'll think I'm mad!"

Simon and Penny came to stay at John Peel's cottage with Penny's puppy, Freddy. They were a blessed leavening in an otherwise heavy dough. Lucky, the fluffy black and white cat, regarded the canine guests with inscrutable politeness, not even complaining when they gobbled up the remains of her meal, which she purposely left for a future hungry moment. She never learned to gobble it up herself to make sure of it; that would have been unmannerly and there was enough crudity round here.

Alex's feet appeared to heal amazingly well after a few weeks. He had been given daily dressings but no painkillers, as requested.

The doctor said, "I don't know what you're doing in this hospital! You should have gone somewhere for your feet, but now they are healed we can't keep you here any longer. Where are you going to go from here?"

That was the problem. Mum presumed Alex would be coming to her. Simon and Penny went to Les for objective advice. He sensed a "mother hen" situation and felt that Alex's best chance of recovery might be with Simon and Penny. Mum was deeply wounded as well as surprised. The three left together, leaving Jess. She was in season and would have caused problems with the other dogs on the farm. Nothing to the problems she was to cause at the cottage, but who could tell?

The party over, Mum and Dandan settled down into life as before, Dandan receiving her share of attention once more. They went to see them at Wicken Clough one day. Simon greeted them.

"How's Alex?" was Mum's first question.

"I don't know where he is," he looked uncomfortable. "I think he went upstairs."

Upstairs? There was a cloakroom. Was he trying to avoid her? He must have known she was here. They would have been waiting for them, sitting in that window, watching the road. You could see cars coming from half a mile away. Did he think it was *her* idea that he should come here and not to her? Did he feel abandoned by her? How could she ever explain to him? But perhaps it was not that? What then?

Alex came into the room and greeted them politely; affectionately? All seemed quite natural and the social occasion passed pleasantly. Penny was not there. She was working.

All this time Jess was still at John Peel's cottage. It was not until the family had left without her that Mum realised how impossible it would be to look after her. Being in season she would have to be shut up, and where could she shut her up? She and Freddy had shared floor space while Simon and Penny had Alex's bed. But that room must now be cleaned up. She could have been left in the front passage, but the milkman came early, and always came right in to leave the milk on the shelf. Jess would escape. Or she could have been left in the scullery, only that door never shut. It was as old as the house and must have been made of green timber and been warped ever since. The kitchen and dining room were out of bounds, she being innocent of any sort of training. Mum didn't fancy the idea of having her in her bedroom.

No, the only thing for it was Dandan's bathroom. Dandan never left her room till Mum brought her a cup of tea. While she was drinking it, Mum prepared her bathroom, turning on the stove and running the hot tap. She could keep a box in there for Jess and remedy any mishaps; open the window briefly and turn up the fan heater full blast.

The first morning of the new routine, Mum came downstairs as usual. Something bright blue caught her eye out of the window. She looked more closely and saw an amazing sight. A little old lady in a bright blue dressing gown was standing by the garden gate, white hair blowing in the breeze. Mum bolted down the stairs and out to the back door.

"What *do* you think you're doing, Dandan?" She never raised her voice to her mother, except when pretended deafness made it inevitable.

"He wanted to go out…"

"But it isn't a 'he'. I explained to you, it is a 'she', and she's in season. We have to keep her shut up."

"He's all right. There's no need to be so cross. He'll come back when I call him."

No sign of Jess. Mum conducted Dandan back to her room; her tea was getting cold. After breakfast she explained the situation again to Dandan, more calmly. But nothing would change her opinion that she was he, and that he should be allowed out when he wanted to go and that he would have come back if she had been left to see to it.

Mary came over presently: "Could you come and get your dog? She's chasing my ducks."

Mum wished she could find a home for the poor creature. She'd always thought it a waste of time, taking a dog for a walk. She'd done too much of it when she was young. But this was Alex's dog, and he was especially attached to her. Had she not sat by the river, waiting for him, for over four hours? That was some test of loyalty. She could not let her down. She might be the mainstay of his recovery. Or would he find her an embarrassment when he saw her again? She could not take the risk. She must look after her. But train her? No, that was Alex's job. It would be an interest for him, and he would need her when he returned to Higher Clough.

Jess's season seemed to go on and on. Luckily, the dogs (who were mostly untrained too) were not much more of a nuisance than usual, though there were more dogs than people in the hamlet.

One evening, Boxing Day, or the next, Alex rang. "Hello. I'm all right. I'm staying with friends."

"Hello, dear. What friends? Where are you?"

"You don't know them, but they are awfully kind people who thought I'd like to ring you up."

"That's lovely, but where are you?"

"I'm not far from that place where we met for a picnic."

"How on earth did you get there?"

95

"I walked."

That was all. It must have been fifty miles! What about his feet? He must have been coming up to her. Thank heaven! Would he be here tomorrow? But he had rung off saying there was food waiting for him. Well, someone had got the Christmas message, and had made him ring her.

But the next call was from Simon, in great distress. Alex had come back yesterday but had stormed out this morning, leaving a trail of devastation behind him. He had left the house early, having taken Simon's keys and wallet and scattered the contents to the winds. Some of his things he still could not find. Finally, he had taken the gate off its hinges and hurled it against the wall, where it shattered. And all this while Alex was hurling abuse at Simon, who felt very wounded indeed after all his hospitality and care these last few weeks.

It was not till later that Alex could explain to Mum that he had been suffering from his Puritanical mood, which had accounted for his thesis, and the religious experience he had had while he was in hospital. This happens to many such patients. They may not actually see God, or hear Him, but they are acutely aware of His presence. Just as, in a dream, one knows it is about a particular person, but they don't always have substance.

In this puritanical mood, Alex felt like an avenging angel, seeing in the fact that Simon and Penny smoked, drank the occasional glass of wine and were, in biblical terms, living in sin as the abomination of Sodom and Gomorrah. His cauldron was already boiling up when Christmas came to remind him of the sorry state of things. Christmas had always been such a wonderful time when all the family was together, when father was alive. And now he had gone: they were in a terrible turmoil.

Mum came down once more, leaving Dandan and Jess in my care, as I'd come for Christmas. She found Simon and Penny waiting for her. There was no news. The police were out looking. Simon proposed that they go down into the village, then, if they hadn't seen him, he and Penny should take the lane, which led by the stream. Mum should go on round and meet them by the bridge. Min would stay at home and take any phone calls. Later Min and Mum took another route, leaving the others to do the chores and man the phone.

When they returned, there had been a call to say that Alex was with friends of Simon's, four or five miles away. The police were already there when they arrived, standing around, waiting for something to happen. Alex was sitting on the sofa, holding forth bout something or other. The couple, mindful of their ten-year-old son, who was sitting next to him, were looking dazed and helpless. There was no need for anyone to make conversation.

Simon and Mum came into the room. Mum had already met these friends, and, moving towards Alex, greeted them cheerfully, as if this were simply a repeat social call. June made some tea. Presently, Mum asked if she might ring the doctor. He was in the surgery. No, he couldn't come out. Mum must bring him in. That might not be so easy. In any case she really wanted to get him back to the hospital he knew. The day was drawing in. If she went down to the surgery first, it would be very late before they could start, even if they were not kept waiting. She told the doctor that she would prefer to attempt to take him north, and that if she did not turn up at his surgery, would he please assume that they had gone to Carlisle?

The policeman was very dubious about letting them go. He thought they might constitute a road hazard. She persuaded him, with a greater show of confidence than she felt, that she could handle the situation. They were off.

All was well until they got halfway up the motorway, when the engine stalled. Surely she'd filled up with petrol? Then she remembered that it had happened before, not long ago, when she had been taking Dandan for her "run". They had had to abandon the car by the roadside, and she had walked a mile to find a taxi to take Dandan home. Twenty miles.

No taxis on the motorway. She must try and attract help. This might have been possible if she could have got out of the car; but if she got out, Alex would get out, and who knew what would happen then? He might decide to cross the road, or start walking, or even take to the fields. It was a dark night. They sat for some moments before Mum remembered what had happened last time. She'd had to wait for some days until Derek, from the Garage, had time to collect the car. He had then reported that there was nothing wrong with it. How embarrassing! And how expensive: just the sort of thing that happens with Dandan. But this was Alex, and the situation was worse. Were they going to be benighted there? Or would the car decide to get going again? Evidently not.

Fortunately, Alex was quite content to sit there, and after ten minutes or so, she tried again. No trouble at all. First touch of a button! As luck would have it, the doctor who knew Alex was on duty when they arrived. Mum explained everything to him.

"But, Mrs Dalglish, I can't take him here."

"You can't?" Mum as aghast. "Why not?"

"You've brought me no doctor's letter. You are a nurse. You know the rules as well as I do: I can't take a patient without a doctor's letter."

Mum had sometimes thanked heaven that this was one branch of medicine where nobody bumbled about red tape. Perhaps she had been lucky.

"Didn't Dr Johnson ring you?"

She had not thought to ask him, but he might have done it; after all, he was more conversant with red tape than she was.

"No. He didn't."

"We've just driven a hundred miles! We can't go back there at this time of night. Do you think Dr Bob would give us one?"

"Yes, you must go and see him and come back to me."

That meant another twenty miles each way – and yet another to get her home. What would the car feel about that? Luckily, the car had no objections. Dr Bob was helpful, as ever, and they approached the hospital once more. This time without a hitch. Alex was received into his 5-star accommodation.

Chapter 12

Warfare

Mum returned to the comfort of a home where supper was ready. I was thinking of staying for the rest of the winter. The gardening work had eased off and the initial flow of students had gained their places at Austin Friars, and it would save on the heating bills. Mum welcomed my company. Alex was likely to be away for a fortnight. But I had a change of heart and went back to Carlisle. I had enjoyed walking Jess, who, miraculously still seemed to be in season. Alex could walk her when he came back. Jess had quite lost the terror she had when she first came. When Mum returned from hospital, that first visit, she'd forgotten all about the dog and found her still cowering under the bed. It had taken a very long time to lure her out with bowls of food, each time a yard further from the bed. She couldn't be tempted downstairs till next day.

When things settled down she came out with Mum one day when she was working in the barn. She got into a habit of hiding in a safe corner and coming in again with Mum at lunchtime. One day, Mum, thinking she'd stay there, as she seemed to want to, left her, and she vanished. So, a closer watch had still to be kept. Then it was noticed that her teats were beginning to swell, as if she were pregnant. Oh dear! Were they too late? Had anything happened while they were out? But there was actually milk there. It must have happened ages ago! Before Alex had her? It was a mystery, and an unwanted nuisance. Alex would be coming out soon, and then what? She was not a very nice dog, Mum thought woefully. Apart from her immoral habits, she had developed a furtive trait, scavenging in every corner, though quite well fed. But then, that's what pregnancy does, perhaps?

Alex hated it when he got back. He felt that he had been humiliated in hospital, being removed speedily from the 5-star end and locked up with all the smokers, having to take medicine like everyone else and live with the down-and-outs. So, this is what he'd fought so hard to avoid? And he'd lost. To come out and find that neither he nor Jess recognised each other, and that she had become, in his absence, this wild and unlovely creature did nothing to help his recovery.

In fact, it was the last thing he needed. He needed to work on himself without the added responsibility of her. He took her for walks and expected standards of behaviour of which she was quite incapable and he could not instill in her. He came to hate her and she was frightened of him. Dandan, who had previously ignored her, if she couldn't get rid of her, now made advances to her, under Alex's nose, which infuriated him even more. He did not need failure at this juncture. He desperately needed success. But where was that to be found?

He was sure that the pills he was supposed to be taking were making him worse. Mum tried to persuade him to take them as directed or talk to Dr Bob about it. He did and persuaded him to reduce the dose, just before the doctor went on holiday. Whether it was a mistake to reduce them – a doctor is always at a disadvantage with such a patient – or whether Alex had made a mistake in the altered dose, no one will ever know, but he became increasingly restless and unhappy.

Mum found a list by his bed one day:

7.30 a.m.	Wait for Mum to bring tea.
	Get up and go to bathroom.
	Get dressed. Put on vest,
	pants, socks, shirt, trousers.
	Put on pullover if cold.
8.00 a.m.	Breakfast. Cornflakes and toast.
	Etc.

Why write such a list? Doesn't it go without saying? Not if you are not quite certain of yourself and you don't want to be caught out.

Mum suddenly remembered the patient at St. Thomas's. She had gone off duty one evening and noticed that he had a policeman sitting by his bed. He was evidently too ill to be questioned. In the morning they had both gone. The man had feigned sleep and when the policeman nodded off, he slipped out of bed and ran right out of the hospital and down the road onto the bridge. He had reached the middle and jumped over before anyone could recover their surprise and stop him. He must have known, poor chap, that he was losing control. It must be a petrifying experience, going out into the void, where no one can reach you: like being the first astronaut, without any training and no guarantee of return, and certainly not of your own choice.

Life was too complicated at John Peel's cottage. There was too much stress. Les must have known how it would be when he sent Alex down to Wicken Clough. It looked as if Mum could not look after both Alex and Dandan. What could she do? Dandan had booked her ticket at birth, and Mum had promised. But how could she turn Alex out?

Alex said bluntly one day, "Either she goes, or I do."

He meant it. A decision had to be made. There could be no hesitation. Dandan was a born survivor. Alex needed her. There was no time to lose. Mum consulted Yellow Pages. They yielded several possibilities, only one of which had a vacancy. It was a double room, but if she was prepared to share…? What? Dandan share? The mind boggled.

"We'll take it, thank you."

"It isn't quite ready yet, but if you are in a hurry, I suggest you come along and see this afternoon, and if you are satisfied, we could have it ready by five o'clock."

"Yes, thank you very much, I'm sure we will like it. We'll be along presently."

They found a beautiful house, too big to remain private, in a well-kept garden with a drive from the lodge gate. This looked promising. They were greeted by a kindly woman, who led them to the available room. It had a large window overlooking the lake. It was fantastic! Dandan approved.

They drove back to John Peel's cottage with lightened hearts.

"It seems a nice place, Moll. If I only have to stay for a week or two, that would be quite all right."

"It's more the manor to which you would like to be accustomed, isn't it?" Mum quipped.

Dandan smiled. "It's nice to see things well kept, isn't it? But I wouldn't want to stay there."

Mum noticed that on the way home that Dandan was not talking much, but she was clicking her fingers and her tongue, as she did when she was "furious-but-not-showing-it". When they got back into the car with her suitcase, she was muttering as she got in, "I must have gone wrong somehow."

The moon came out, too large again, and still threatening? Evil? Mum suddenly felt, with great certainty, that she had no choice but to bring Dandan away at this time.

She returned to find Alex, not settled, as she had hoped now Dandan was gone, but still uneasy. At least he was there.

Dandan was very happy as it turned out. She felt herself well able to hold her own with the other old ladies, some of them much younger than her, who needed a four-pronged stick or frame to get about with, whereas she could afford to leave her stick behind at a pinch. And they were so dull! They had nothing to say for themselves. She at least read her book; they never even read. (Dandan's did not need changing and she was quite happy to read each page over and over again. But that was not the point.) Her biggest triumph was sitting next to the only man on the premises. Surely there was a fight over that? For Dandan, no doubt, it was a pushover. He was in fact something of a celebrity as a photographer, and wanted to show Dandan his photographs, but she was not particularly interested.

Sometimes Mum and Alex went together to see her and sometimes she went alone, which was less constrained. Dandan was away for five weeks, always with the promise that she could come home as soon as possible. But it was not a success. The old jealousies and irritations grew worse. In his desultory mood Alex would talk with Dandan in her room. She had no understanding of his needs and thought her treasured Book of Daily Light would solve all his problems. It is a strange thing that religion, when not properly understood can be absolutely lethal. Mum had found this before with me. She tried to explain to Dandan and asked her *please* not to discuss the matter with him. After another spell of torment Mum encouraged him to go off for a walk, quietly, by himself. He went, and Mum, being so riled by Dandan's obstinacy and so genuinely frightened of Alex's frenzy, opened the Rayburn door and threw in the offending book.

She felt quite weak at the knees, as if she were on the brink of hellfire, herself. Really, Dandan would have to go, and soon. The home she had quite enjoyed would not take her back. Mum rang the surgery to see if they knew of anyone else? They gave her a couple of names. One she'd tried before, and one was quite nearby. They'd often passed it, noticing the sign, "CHRISTIAN..." So that was a rest home, was it? That would be very handy. Alex came back from his walk and insisted on driving them to see it.

"No, you stay here," he said authoritatively. "I'll see to this."

In her younger days Dandan would have swept him aside and marched in, but she was not sure what was going on. Mum held her breath. She was not going to upset him more than need be, and it would be interesting to see what would happen.

Alex pulled the bell vigorously and a youngish man came to the door, wearing a carpenter's apron. The women stayed in the car, Mum all ears.

"Good morning, are you a Christian establishment?"

"Er, I suppose so. Why do you ask?"

"I'm looking for somewhere for my grandmother. I think this will suit her very well."

"Hang on a minute! We don't take people here."

"Oh, isn't this some sort of rest home? I was told it was."

"No, sorry, old man. We've not been here long. I think the people who were here before may have had a home. We're just altering the place, as you see."

Alex pricked up his ears. Alterations. Now that was interesting.

"Mind if I have a look?"

"Be my guest."

The two disappeared inside, or would have done if Mum had not extricated herself from the back seat in time to join the conversation and suggest that time was pressing. They drove back, Alex not too pleased to have been interrupted. Mum went to the kitchen to get some lunch ready and heard loud voices coming from Dandan's room. She rushed in to find Alex towering over Dandan who shrank into her chair.

"Why can't you find anywhere to go Dandan? Nobody wants you! Even St. Peter doesn't want you. We don't want you here. Why can't you just go away?"

Louder and louder. Mum had never thought that she could feel sorry for Dandan. But this was terrible.

"Alex," she grabbed hold of his arm. "Alex, you mustn't say things like that. Remember, Dandan's a frail old woman."

For answer, he seized her stick and smashed it in two.

"Come on, Alex, please come and help me make lunch."

"No. I can't come out there. I'm going to have this out with Dandan!"

In fact, he had shot his bolt, and lost interest. Mum was able to rescue the lunch before it burned, and they ate it. Alex wandered off.

The surgery, as luck would have it, had heard of yet another possible home since she rang this morning, and this one was only half finished. They had a choice of rooms available now.

At last Dandan and Mum were alone.

"Alex has gone mad," Dandan declared with the utmost indignation possible (as if this were worse than not taking one's cap off to a lady).

"Yes. I've been trying to tell you for a long time."

For the first time in her life Dandan had been frightened. At a dinner party she was giving in Mobberley the butler informed her that one of the villagers was wielding a knife over his wife. She went straight to the scene and said, "Young man, give me that knife!" Shocked, he handed it over.

But now, she asked Mum to escort her down the passage and she had the grace to ask Mum if she would be all right. With Alex still in charge, they made their way eventually to the rest home where Dandan was seated on a comfortable chair in the hall, while Alex and Mum were taken round the amenities. It was a very nice, purpose-built place, a complete contrast to the other, but with its own merits: everybody around looked happy, and it seemed that many of the staff had undertaken graduate courses on geriatrics. The atmosphere was kindly.

The sister showed them the bathrooms and said, "Of course we will help your grandmother with her bath." Alex caught Mum's eye and they both burst out laughing.

"I don't think you quite know what you're taking on!"

It was some months since Dandan had stopped taking a bath. Since she began to find it a rather difficult manoeuvre, she had opted out. It was not for the lack of any offer to help, but Dandan never needed help. And a bath was a very private thing. Human bodies were such nasty things, as she frequently commented. They had no cause for complaint, so they took the easy way. Mum always believed that Dandan won the oncoming battle.

Chapter 13

Carried Feet First

Alex settled down after she had gone, but was still borderline for a week. They visited Dandan together, Mum on tenterhooks. After five minutes she began asking him all about Jess, his sorest spot. Mum rose.

"It's time to go," she said coolly, and they left.

"I'd have been all right on my own," Alex said, feeling rather foolish. "It's only you that makes an atmosphere. She's all right really."

"I'm sure it's deliberate. Don't tell me she doesn't know what she's doing."

Two days later he went again, on his own. Dandan was delighted to see him, greeting him with one of her most radiant smiles and revelling in showing him off to the other old ladies at teatime. She was not a deserted old woman! Her realm was still intact! Privately they chatted and Alex came home, sober minded and pleased to have withstood his ordeal.

"You were right." he said. "She tried every trick to try and break me. I shan't go again."

He had to see the doctor the next day and told him that he and his mother were thinking of moving back to his farmhouse. They supposed that they could find somewhere nearby, in Lancashire, for Dandan.

"Don't do that," he said. "Leave your grandmother where she is. She is very well looked after. You go, and good luck to you. It is someone else's turn."

Mum could not believe her luck! "The doctor says..." She had always thought he had the right idea: he drove a Mini, not a Rolls, like all the St. Thomas's pundits.

One evening she and Alex had an argument, Alex saying that he was going out. He was in a rather blustery mood and she thought it would be better not to. It was no use saying "No" straight out; subtlety is a good tool, but not one with which Mum was skillful. She thought she had better take the keys out of the car, but was too obvious and too slow. As he raced to the door he pushed her over. Before she could recover herself he had gone. She was not hurt, so much as shocked. In all her experience with me, she had managed to keep pace. She was getting old. Once when she heard me go out in the night, she had raced down in her nighty, had caught up with me and got in the car. She mustn't lose sight of me in that condition. We had driven around for a quarter of an hour or so and I'd simmered down and gone back to bed.

She was getting old. Al was too quick for her and too big! Six foot three and well built. He had not hurt her – yet. What of the future? And where had he gone? Was he now trying to get back to Wicken Clough, as he had tried to get back here from there? Would he have enough petrol? Was he safe to drive?

The telephone rang: the local police.

"We have your son here. What are we to do with him?"

She had had a similar call once before when he had walked into town and helped himself to some sweets in Woolworths. Then his conscience had suggested that he give himself up. He had had a most enjoyable chat with the sergeant, who rang Mum, who came and fetched him.

But this was different. He had gone off in a huff. It was late; the nights were always the worst, and anyway, he had got the car. She could not fetch him if she wanted to. The sergeant said he had better call the doctor and, reluctantly, she agreed: his own doctor, who would be less traumatic. Doctor Bob could hardly appreciate this doubtful compliment when he travelled out to this distant station, sparsely manned at night. Alex saw no reason why he should go back to hospital, and they had to do for Alex what it took six men to do for me. However, it was he who went in the end.

During the next week I went over the top at Warwick Square and found myself back in the same hospital, so Mum's days were spent visiting us all. She could visit Dandan on her own now; heaven knew when she would see her again after Alex was released. Alex and I were at either end of Garlands. Mum did not feel it would help either of us to know. Dandan was at Rosehill, Penrith, so it was a round journey of seventy miles daily. Dandan had settled in remarkably well. A visiting cousin from South Africa had located her and given her great joy. Apart from the treat of a special visitor she had the courage to adapt to any circumstances, wherever she went she found people to love and admire her. Her tragedy was that Mum was not one of them. Really, she was better off at Rosehill!

In due course, having been visited by Les and some of his friends, I returned to Warwick Square, and Alex returned to John Peel's cottage. He was not happy there. Jess was still a problem. It was obviously a false pregnancy, as there was no natural progress in her condition. Poor unhappy little creature! They tried to find another home for her, but without success.

"What? Not house-trained, at that age? And a phantom pregnancy, you say? Not a hope."

Jess solved her own problem, by running away one day when walking with Alex.

Alex himself said, "Couldn't we go to Higher Clough now?"

Mum said, "I need time to sort everything out here. But we'll go today for a picnic, and we'll move down as soon as we can."

Alex would dearly have liked to shake the dust off his feet and get on back to his own home. It was a lovely early spring day in 1985: new lambs, green leaves and daffodils. They started off very happy, chatting of this and that. Whether he had forgotten to take his medicine before they went, or whatever reason, Alex began to boil up. He wanted to call in at Wicken Clough to collect a sun hat; but, by the time they came in sight, Alex was driving like

Jehu, roaring up the rough drive at eighty miles an hour, doing a sharp turn at the top, and stopping inches away from the building.

Simon came out, somewhat alarmed, and while Alex was inside finding his hat, Mum hurriedly asked him to send the doctor to Higher Clough. They could not have chosen a worse day for their picnic. At that very moment, unbeknown to Mum, Simon was awaiting the arrival of Carol, Charles's wife, and her mother, from Australia. Mum knew of the visit but not the timing. Of course they had to meet in the lane. Alex was driving and Mum hoped that he, not expecting them, would not recognise them; but he did. They all stopped, but what was there to say?

Their lunch party must have been sadly spoiled, with all the arrangements to be made. Simon had been in the Burnley Police Force for a while and contacted some of his former colleagues, so that when the doctor came they were there as reinforcement. Alex saw them come and hospitably offered them tea. He left them to get on with it while he went through to the sitting room. They heard wood snapping. Mum, peeping in, saw him breaking up a small table as firewood. She felt very uncomfortable since she had said nothing to him about the doctor. She suspected that he knew what it was all about: she felt his terror.

The doctor came with Simon to show him the way. He did his paperwork and spoke to Alex. Then it was time to go. What happened to the injection? The four policemen carried Alex, feet first, across rough ground until they reached their van. Mum would remember till her dying day, the heart breaking cries, receding into the distance, as they bore him away, knowing that she had betrayed him.

Simon too, was distraught.

"To think that a man can be carried out of his own house like that, against his will!" Did he wonder if it could happen to him? (It could happen to anyone, but there is no need.)

110

Simon accompanied Mum to the Burnley Hospital, having collected a few things. Then he took her back to join Carol and her mother at Wicken Clough. They made plans for Carol and her mother to visit John Peel's cottage for a couple of nights, before Mum had to dismantle everything and pack up. Neither had seen it and Mum wanted so much to show them the beauties of her part of the world. There was no alternative but to sell it if she could. And in all probability she would have just a fortnight in which to do it. She rang the hospital to ask the doctor if he thought it would affect Alex adversely if she were unable to visit.

"Suit yourself!" She could feel him shrug his shoulders.

"Can you tell me how long he is likely to be in?"

"It's impossible to say."

That's a fat lot of help, Mum thought to herself, but supposed it was all he could say.

Packing up and selling was not an easy matter at the best of times, but Mum was embroiled in complicated negotiations to acquire an extra piece of land to provide, possibly ample garden space, but minimally, space for a compulsory new septic tank for one pair of cottages, and parking space for the other pair. Without this acquisition, neither pair was viable. Then she had Dandan's effects to sort out, the remains of Alex's and mine and all her own; to say nothing of the furnishings of the holiday cottages.

One buyer emerged and halved the problems at a stroke. He only wanted one of a pair, which was indivisible, but if Mum would accept delayed payment he would take over the negotiations enabling her to extend her remaining boundary. Mum had no doubt that her bank manager would be as happy to support him as herself, and the problem was solved.

Amid all the chaos of removal, Les and I came together to remind her that it was Mothering Sunday. He and I had seen each other every week for nearly a year. He'd analysed my paintings and dreams; I often did his garden for him; we'd go for walks, quoting Shakespeare to each other. We developed a deep friendship. I saw him as my mentor. When he asked me to move in with him I said candidly, "I cannot love you, but I will care for you till your last breath."

When Mum heard of our proposed partnership she became Mrs Bennet in *Pride and Prejudice*, full of notions of acquiring a son-in-law. I did not see it that way: he was forty-three years older than me, and six inches shorter. It was a thunderbolt for Mum, but also a solution to my long-term prospects, to which she had not given much thought lately. Les agreed to let me stay with him keeping my maiden name. It showed the true quality of the man, in that he was highly respected in his neighbourhood and much sought after as a counsellor. He had laid himself open at least to raised eyebrows.

I moved into his comfortable bungalow together with the baby grand piano and rugs. The only casualty was Les's cleaning lady, Mrs Miller, who took off in disgust, but soon returned, becoming as devoted to me as to Les.

In the meantime, Mary reported that Jess had been found but that the farmer did not want to keep her, nor would he put her down. Mum must fetch her. She had hoped so much that the poor little creature would have found herself a happy home, but it was not to be. She would have to take her to be put down.

Jess was pleased to see her, which cut her to the quick. She thanked the farmer's wife for looking after her and asked if she knew of anyone? Of course she didn't. There was nothing for it but the vet. Together they went and sat in the waiting room. Jess seemed to know what they were waiting for. Her eyes were alert, hair standing on end; she shivered. The receptionist came out.

"It will be five pounds, please."

Mum had ten and handed it over. She didn't want any change: what was money on such an occasion?

"Will you come in, please?"

The vet, a kindly man, put a mask over Jess's muzzle, speaking comfortably as he did so.

"Will you wait outside, please?" The receptionist opened the door.

Dazed, Mum sat again outside. What was there to wait for? Presently, the girl came out again and handed her five pounds change. Mum felt as if she had been stabbed. Money! Was this what Judas felt like when they gave him his thirty pieces of silver? She left the surgery in a haze of tears, howling and driving dangerously all the way home.

Chapter 14

The Void

Alex was released without reference to the convenience of his reception. Simon rang to say that the hospital was expecting him to fetch Alex for lunch next day. He would keep him till Mum came. Could she manage lunch? She had better try. Since Alex's recent exit from Wicken Clough as an outraged prophet of old, after all Simon's care of him, things had not been easy between the two brothers. They were still not easy over lunch and Mum began to wonder if he were really ready to come home.

Simon had done his very best, not only visiting, though not always welcome, but he had tried to get Higher Clough warm and welcoming after six months of winter neglect. He had had only partial success, since he was unable to unravel the secrets of how everything worked. Alex had been determined that no vandal should get into the place in his absence, and squander his resources.

At last Alex was home. There was nowhere else he would long to be. He was safe. He opened the door for Mum. They walked through the barn and into the kitchen. It was beautifully tidy, clean tablecloth, nothing lying about. But it felt cold and damp. Alex turned on the electricity and Mum made a cup of tea – always the first thing to do, at any time of arrival.

Inspection of the premises was depressing. There were a couple of burst pipes, a new phenomenon for Alex, since he had only installed his bore hole last summer, and had no experience of running water, as a householder. The bursts meant that the Aga could not be lit until they were mended. Alex had done all the plumbing himself but was in no fit state to attempt it now, so a plumber had to be found. At last all was well and the Aga could be lit, but first it must be filled with oil.

Owing to the shoestring budget, Alex had not yet acquired an oil tank. No wagon could get up his lane, so he filled a number of five-gallon drums, and from these, with funnel and hose, he kept a small tank filled. Luckily the drums were not all empty and Alex soon coaxed the Aga into life. With the help of electric blankets and a calor gas fire they warmed up. But alas for Alex's pictures: those on the walls and others in the big box under his bed – all he said were ruined beyond hope. The walls were damp, some, streaming, some with plaster lifting, some just mouldy. It was a sorry sight. The paper on which his pastel drawings were done was all crinkled.

"Could we use an iron to flatten them?" Mum asked, as desolate as he to think of his life's work lying in ruins, and what chance of his ever doing anything more, whether as an artist or a builder?

"No," he said finally. "It's hopeless. It will never be any good."

And so he felt, for six months, obediently taking his pills and attending the clinic. He seemed to be in a sort of trance, never smiling, not complaining, not by any means the Alex she knew and loved, though it was Alex and she still loved him of course. She tried her best to give him hope, hope of his own recovery at least. Without that, he would never recover. That she knew.

Higher Clough had lost its enchantment for him. He spoke of selling up and starting afresh, somewhere where neither of them was known. The hope was that the price fetched for Higher Clough would buy a smaller property, and leave enough to invest for income. The asking price was based on former projections, and the project was incomplete. The estate agent came up with an assessment that Alex found positively insulting. They decided to stay put.

It was hard to find any encouragement. Alex had no energy. It was difficult to fill each day with interest, without

115

taxing the brain. Alex used to walk three miles to Barnoldswick, buy a paper, visit an old friend, Elsie, who would give him a cup of tea and a rest while they chatted, then walk home for lunch. It was as much as he could do, but with the rest, he could manage it. Other days he would walk over the top to visit Stan, who had persuaded him to buy Jess.

It was very difficult for him now to understand how Alex could have allowed such a fate to overtake any animal of his, but he trusted his own judgment and believed that Alex was neither wanton nor cruel. He became a wonderful friend to Alex, one with whom, as he recovered, he was able to discuss every subject under the sun.

"What *is* the matter with him?" Stan asked Mum diffidently one day. Alex had gone for a paper and he found her on her own.

"He had a mental breakdown, you know. That's why he could not look after that dog. He's not the man to let that happen if he could help it."

"How does it affect him exactly?"

"Well, it's a disease which concerns mood swing, and energy. He had tremendous bursts of energy, running miles over frozen ground, then, before his feet can have had time to heal properly, he was off, cross-country walking, up to fifty miles a day. Now he's got no energy at all. It is as if his power-house were shattered."

"It's sad, isn't it? He is such a strong, good-looking fellow, and he's made such a wonderful place here. I remember walking past this place when it was derelict and the roof fallen in! Is he going to be all right, do you think?"

Mum sighed. "I very much hope so. I've always maintained that there must be a cure, but no one has ever confirmed it. My daughter has suffered from similar breakdowns for years, but I still hope. At least Alex can rest peacefully now, in his own home. I think he may have been harder hit than Sally ever was, because he has been fighting it for so long, and so bravely, that defeat, when it came, was all the harder to bear."

Stan rose to his feet. "Thank you for telling me," he said. "I hope he will keep coming to see me. I enjoy his company. And you must come with him sometimes?"

Apart from walking, and once a week shopping in the supermarket, which both found exhausting, Mum and Alex often went out in the car, "burning petrol" in the country lanes. Otherwise, they filled the hours sitting on the sofa in the kitchen. Sometimes they would chat, dreaming little dreams together, or trying to find some light on their situation. Alex had an excellent music centre and some beautiful tapes, which he would play when Mum and Dandan had visited from John Peel's cottage: piano music by Chopin, and Tchaikovsky, which they both loved. But it was too poignant for Alex's present condition. The television programmes too, had to be severely censored, as indeed did the paper he had laboriously brought. News seemed mostly to consist of violence, disaster and pornography, and few programmes were much better. If that was what the public wanted, it did not speak very highly of public taste. Sports programmes Alex enjoyed. There was no cerebral strain and he had always been a sportsman himself. Tennis, snooker, bowls and boxing whiled away many an hour of box watching. Perhaps it was the individual performance that fascinated; football had little appeal.

And still it was difficult to overcome the settling gloom. Mum was determinedly cheerful, until the family said: "You're making him worse, Mother!"

"But if I don't keep cheerful, I too will crack."

There was nothing to be seen from a comfortable position inside the house, which had narrow mullioned windows. The fantastic view to the north could be seen when standing up, either in the kitchen, or from a small window in Mum's bedroom above it. Above that there was an unfinished box room with no window at all. Now, if there were a window there it would command the most fabulous view for miles around! Mum persuaded Alex to consider getting men in to install a window there. The estimate would have bought the whole house, not long since, but times had changed.

The resulting room with its comfortable settee in front of the breathtaking view fifty miles to the north, and the summer sunsets, became known as "the retreat", and was infinitely comforting to their bruised spirits. Before the new window was put in, they used to go sometimes to sit in Simon's big window, with its grand open view across to where Charles and Carol had once lived, before emigrating. Simon was on his own these days and back in his wagon, so out all day. Mum took the opportunity of making piles of sandwiches for him, leaving them in his fridge. She was sure that otherwise he would forget to eat.

Simon's fortieth birthday was approaching. He and Min had been over to celebrate Charles's two years ago. It would be terrific if he could return the compliment; but Australia is not just across the way. It was too much to hope. All the same, a party was called for. Offers of help were turned down. This was going to be a proper job, put out to caterers, who fulfilled all his hopes and relieved the family of responsibility.

The day was slightly marred for Simon by the fact that while driving he was stopped by the police. But Charles, arriving unannounced, turned the incident to good effect by briefing a "kiss-o-gram" girl to come to the party dressed as a policewoman. A great success! Mum and Alex arrived in time for this event and stayed an hour. It was something of a strain for Alex, not knowing any of Simon's friends and not drinking. It was a much more rowdy form of life than he had grown used to.

Next day he felt, probably unjustifiably, that his brothers despised him as an idler. He went to the job centre and realised that there was no job he could even apply for, let alone hold down. It depressed him further. The party over, and a couple of days later Simon was back at work and Charles needed taking to the airport. Who should take him but Mum and Alex? Charles drove there, but being unfamiliar with this airport, Alex and Mum lost their way

118

home. For one used to a quiet life, driving in heavy traffic on the wrong road is an unnerving experience, and Alex was already disturbed by the party and the excursion to the job centre.

It was unfortunate that at this particular moment Mum's property problems had to rear their ugly head. She had left them in the hands of lawyers to sort out, hardly daring to think about them, let alone mention them, since any look of anxiety on her face worried Alex and set him back. The moment had come when she could ignore the matter no longer. The buyer of the middle cottage who had made a handsome offer three months ago rang to say that her lawyer had advised her not to wait any longer for the contract. Mum had telephoned her own lawyer who said he was waiting to hear from the first buyer's lawyer about the extended boundary. (How is it that the kind of man one would choose as a friend is never the kind one needs to get things done?)

Clearly nothing would happen unless she made it. It should be simple enough to call on her lawyer, collect the required form, take it to the first buyer for his signature – he had agreed to meet her at his lawyer's office – and take the signed document over to the second buyer's lawyer. But "the little dog wouldn't get over the stile".

The plan went without a hitch until they met the first buyer, whose ideas had changed over the months. They had agreed that if successful in negotiating for the extra land, she could have as much as she wanted, giving her space for several cars, and himself access through to the rear. Now, however, he had been advised that he should claim possession, giving her access but no extra space. There was an argument; it was lunch time, so they agreed to return after lunch, having had time to think it over. There was no further sign of the buyer. His lawyer refused to see Mum. She waited, and made it clear that she was prepared to go on waiting until he was ready to see her. Alex was unhappy but not protesting. After a while the receptionist told her:

"There is no point waiting. Your document has been posted."

"It can't be posted! It would not have left the office till five o'clock."

"We have our own postal services."

"But where has it been posted? It's not been signed yet."

"It has been sent to your lawyer."

This was palpably untrue, as later transpired, but what else could Mum do but accept defeat? This controversial exercise was the last straw for Alex. He hardly slept that night, his sleep pattern being already broken since the party. All day he was restless. He wandered about in the house or outside, unable to settle anywhere. He sat by a pile of gravel and threw pebbles at random: one hit the kitchen window and cracked it. Mum put her head out of the back door.

"How about a cup of coffee?"

"Good idea."

He sat for a few minutes and drank it, but was soon on the move again. He started exploring, looking in drawers. He came across an old school photograph, a group of some seventy boys, little bigger than a postcard. He looked at it for a long time and showed it to Mum in the half-light through the mullioned windows.

"Which one am I?"

To Mum they looked identical, her sight not being what it was. She picked one.

"No." He was disappointed, crestfallen even. "Try again."

Mum looked long and earnestly. Clearly it was important to get it right. But alas, she was wrong again. This was too much for Alex. Even his own mother didn't know him. He had lost his identity. The void, never far away in these last few months, now engulfed him completely. He rushed out screaming into his car. And that, in fact, is where this story started.

Chapter 15

House Smash

The hospital staff were quite pleased to see Alex, sorry of course, that he should have broken down again, but full of admiration that he had stayed out so long. Mum visited every day. I had always been a gannet on such occasions but Alex wanted nothing but orange juice. His medication made him thirsty not hungry. Nothing would induce me to take Largactil; nothing would induce him to take lithium carbonate. He was there for a fortnight, before running the gauntlet of the health committee, who decided whether or not he was fit to go out. Before he left he was told that he must report monthly for a check-up and regular injection. He protested. He was told that if he did not comply he would become a cabbage for the rest of his life. What a prospect! But was this not, in fact, just what he had been for the last six months? The doctor was not pleased. He could not force him. He gave him his prescription for the pills he must take at home: Largactil 150mg four times daily. He had been given 100mg while in hospital, nominally four times daily, but in fact only three times, since he was, with permission, allowed out in the afternoons, thereby missing the fourth dose. That meant that he was now on double the dose to which he was accustomed.

In the meantime, Mum, almost totally inert since the scramble of exodus, saw her chance to do something to make the place more like home. While Alex was around it was impossible to do anything without making ripples, which might delay his recovery. He was incapable of working himself, and if she were to try, he would hate it on two scores: he could not bear to see her working when he could not; and he could not bear to see her making a mess or spoiling his own wonderful project! But now he was away and could not actually see her, surely there must be something she could do which he would have to admit was an improvement? Something to make him feel that all was not lost and that it was still possible to dream?

She rang a man who had done work for Simon and explained the situation.

"First, we need a cattle grid. We were waiting till we could afford one, but we'd have to get a new gate now, anyway, so we might as well go for the grid. Can you help us with that?"

"Sure. I've got some second hand pipes from a demolition site. I thought they might come in handy for a cattle grid. Of course, a new one would cost you two or three hundred pounds, but I'll weld these up for you and they won't cost much."

"That's grand. I hadn't really started thinking about costs. I always find that if you get on and do what has to be done, the costs somehow look after themselves. There never seems to be any money, but they usually do!"

With this rather chancy prospect of repayment, Derek applied himself with a will. It was a good cause and he liked it. With the cattle grid in place, he turned his attention to the hall. It had always seemed rather desolate to Mum, coming in through the dilapidated front door into the barn, with all its great height, high-piled building junk, cobwebs and gloom, before reaching the warmth of the kitchen. With a few concrete blocks and another doorway for access to the barn, a welcoming hall could be made. Mum was aware that this would spoil Alex's one-time dream of a picture gallery with mosaic floor. But what price that dream now? If the day ever came when he could think of putting into practice his killer whale splashing in water, he could demolish her hall, and welcome. In the meantime, there was much to be said for a little practical comfort.

"Derek, do you know of anyone who could do a bit of walling?"

The retaining wall between the kitchen garden and the western gable had yet to be built, and the high plateau was falling down, adding to the difficulties of walking round the house.

"My brother's a farmer. I reckon he could do a bit."

"Do you think he could tackle this mess?"

"Sure. I'll ask him."

The next day both he and Donald came to work after morning milking. Between the three of them they had given the place a new lease of life with which to greet Alex's return.

Mum had said nothing to him about it. If he had not approved, the worst thing would have been to be left to fester, before he could see for himself. As it was he was already feeling pretty pleased with himself having passed through the gauntlet without yielding over the proposed injection. He had stood his ground in front of all of them, a heroic feat for a man in a mental hospital, who is entirely at the mercy of the doctors and made to realise it.

The look on Alex's face when he opened the door into the new hall was reward enough for all the risk and hard work. This was the old Alex, the enthusiast, whom she feared she had lost forever. It was wonderful! They were both ecstatic – not euphoric: there is a world of difference in manic-depressive illness. The world was once more beautiful and full of hope.

They walked round the garden, admiring Donald's new wall and making plans for their future garden, until Alex said, "I can't take any more; my head is aching."

Nothing could spoil this homecoming. It was not just the fact of coming out of hospital; it was the resurrection of the real man, who had, for six months been as one dead.

It didn't last.

The fact was that his medication was about right when he came out of hospital. Maybe the momentary excitement of his return warranted an increase. On his arrival there was a letter telling him that his GP no longer wished to have him on his list, which made him feel rejected, at a vulnerable moment. And he had been told that the psychiatric district nurse, to whom he had become accustomed, was no longer available to him. These things added together were disturbing enough to warrant an increased dosage, so that no ill effects were noticeable at first.

The new psychiatric nurse called and introduced himself. Alex told him of his increased medication, feeling aggrieved to be stepped up, when all he wanted was to come off the pills altogether. He was sure that the doctor had put up his dose to spite him, since he wouldn't fall for the injection.

"Oh, dear no! He would never do a thing like that. The doctor knows what he is talking about. If he wants you to take 150mg four times a day, then that's the dose you should take."

In any case, it was not in the man's power to alter the dose. Alex was depressed. He no longer smiled. The men who came back to finish plastering irritated him. How could he pay them? Life became a dead weight once more. Mum, at her wits' end to find something for him to do which would please him, suggested that they should come and see Les and me.

As soon as they arrived it was apparent that I was hypomanic. Les would know how to handle me, but what sort of effect was it going to have on Alex? It was the worst possible thing that could have happened. Alex was depressed enough to start with. Seeing me like this when we'd all thought I was out of the woods must surely make him sink through the floor? Mum was surprised and delighted that this was not so! We all enjoyed the visit.

Mum was puzzled. She felt sure that Alex must realise I was over the top, and surely he must mind about it? In fact, he did mind, very much but the effect was to disturb him, signifying the need for an increased dose to bring him back to normal, rather than depress him. Neither I nor Mum understood this precarious balance and he remained very unsettled for another week. During this time he slept badly, helped, inadequately, by Temazepan tablets. He would wander round the house at night, fortunately, no further. Mum, who hardly dared to sleep, would sense, sometimes, that he was outside her room, rather than hear him.

"Alex?"

He opened the door.

"Come and sit with me."

He came in and sat on her bed, holding hands.

"I couldn't sleep."

"Did you take your pills?"

"Yes."

He wandered round the room, looking at all her photographs, her "Rogues Gallery". It covered all stages of family life. He was deep in thought, seeing again old memories; remembering old dreams, and back to the present.

"What about a cup of tea?"

"Not yet."

Mum longed for sleep, but it was no good hurrying him. If he were flustered, it would only make it harder for him to get off again to sleep himself.

"Do you want a cup? I'll go and make you one, if you like."

"Well, there's an idea! Yes, I'd love one, thank you."

"I'll take another couple of sleeping pills while I'm about it."

Just the ticket, Mum thought; it would have been no good for her to suggest it, but it looked as if he might really go back to sleep.

They spent several nights, on the edge, like this, until Mum decided that she must get in touch with the psychiatric nurse. Alex was getting worse and she really thought that he was heading for hospital again. The nurse rang back to say that he had managed to get Alex's appointment at the clinic brought forward from Thursday next week to Tuesday this week.

"But don't you understand!" Mum was aghast. "Next week is no good at all! He needs to go to hospital now."

"I'm sorry, there's nothing I can do about it."

"Well, who can? What about our new doctor, Dr Arkwright?"

"Yes, you could try him."

She was lucky enough to speak with him direct.

"As it happens, I am coming out your way this afternoon. I'll look in."

He didn't come till seven o'clock, by which time Alex was like a coiled spring. Mum, for his sake, was trying to pretend nothing was the matter. They had a pleasant chat over the inevitable cup of tea. Dr Arkwright hardly knew either of them and wondered what all the fuss was about. Mum was a little scared of Alex's unpredictability should she threaten him openly with hospital, so hoped that Dr Arkwright would take the initiative. How could he, poor chap? It was not till he said goodbye and shook hands, that he could see the smallest grounds for anxiety. Alex's hand nearly pulverised his with manic strength.

Mum should not have hesitated. Alex knew very well that he had to go to hospital, and the fact that *they* didn't get on with the job worried him. Instead of going to bed when the time came, he took Mum's car (his own was already in dock), and went. Perhaps it was the relief after being on tenterhooks night and day for two weeks that dulled Mum's brain. She could not think where he could have gone to; he did not need to look for her, he was already at home. Surely, he wouldn't go to Simon at this time of night? Anyway, Mum could not ring him, if he had not been disturbed already. There was nothing she could do, only wait.

Then it struck her. Of course! He would go to hospital! Much as he hated the idea, he would do what he knew to be right. She rang the hospital and was put through to the psychiatric wing.

"It's Mrs Dalglish. Has Alex come to you by any chance?"

"Oh, yes! He's just been in."

"Did you say he'd been in? Is he not still with you?"

"No, he's gone now."

"But do you mean to say you let him *go*?"

"Yes, we have no authority to keep him."

"But did you not see that he needed to go back in, and that he realised the fact, and actually brought himself in?"

"Well, I'm sorry, but there's nothing we can do."

"Where did he go from you?"

"I don't know, but he can't have gone far: he said something about not being able to start his car."

"We live ten miles away! How do you expect him to get home, without a car, and in his present state?"

"I'm sorry I can't help you."

Where could he possibly have gone? Of course: the police.

"I'm ringing to report that my son is missing. He should be in hospital really, but he's just been there and been turned away. I understand that his car has broken down and he will therefore be unable to get home. He needs looking after. I suppose he has not called on you?"

"No, madam, we have not heard from him. Ah! Wait a minute. He has just driven up in his car."

"I thought he might. Would it be possible for you to keep him for the night?"

"Oh no, madam, we cannot detain anyone who has not committed an offence." And of course he had the car. There was a pause.

"Hold on a moment...ah, yes. It seems he has just assaulted one of my officers, so we shall be able to offer him our hospitality after all!"

"And would you be able to take him along to the hospital in the morning?"

"We will do that, madam, certainly."

Thank God for the police, at least. Poor old Al, he'd tried hard. But he hadn't got his medication with him. Mum took a Mogadon tablet and slept, as she had dared not sleep for a fortnight. She awoke to a thunderous racket.

All the doors in the house were forcibly banged and torn open and banged again. There was a noise of shattered glass and china and heavy footsteps pounding on the stairs. Mum's heart beat loudly. Fear crept up her neck. She breathed heavily. She knew Alex would never hurt her when he was himself. He was a gentle being. Now he was certainly not himself. She cowered under the bedclothes. He stormed into the room, but did not come near her. He grumbled a bit and went out, to her great relief. The relief didn't last long, however. There was an earsplitting crash.

My God, Mum thought, he's gone through the tall landing window! She could not lurk safely in bed any longer. She got up, put on her dressing gown and went out into the passage. The window was intact. But something had made that noise. She went down to the kitchen where the noise was subsiding at last. A terrible sight greeted her, but at least Alex was alive. He was standing, still in his cap and jacket, surrounded by broken glass and crockery – which Mum had thought unbreakable. The cupboard doors were smashed; the dining room door would need repairing, and to top it all, he had found the deep-fry pan and thrown it on the floor. It had been full. It was not safe to walk anywhere. Where do you start?

"Shall I make some coffee?" she asked mildly.

He made no answer, so she found two unbroken cups and boiled the kettle. He was in a rage still, but quieter now. She handed him his coffee, and the rage broke out again. With a look of hatred, he threw the coffee over her, and the cup on the floor. Then, seizing the heavy old kitchen table, he flung it over on its side. He then rushed out of the house, as if, in spite of that alien look, he knew he might hurt her and feared to do it. She didn't try to stop him. What would have been the use?

But what was he doing here? How had he come to surprise her? She thought him safely tucked up in the police station, or back in hospital? She rang the police station.

"I thought you were going to deliver my son to the hospital? What went wrong?"

"Nothing went wrong, I assure you. We took him there."

"But he's just been in here, smashing the place up!"

"He was definitely taken to hospital this morning and handed over."

"Well, I must get hold of a doctor. He is the only person who can provide the necessary yard of red tape to let him in, apparently. Thank you very much. I'm sorry if I was rude. And incidentally, he's out and about in the meantime. Let's hope he doesn't get into any further trouble."

Mum never knew how eventually he reached his destination. She could not visit him at once since he had taken the car. It now lay with a broken axle, having been driven at speed over a pavement. Mercifully, there had been no pedestrians at the time. A good friend, who had bought Charles's Garage, came to the rescue, lending her a car while he took hers in for repair. She visited on the second day, but not before a fellow patient had kindly written a letter for him. He looked dreadful when she saw him: he was in bed, hardly knowing her, talking deliriously as if from that other world. He must have been very close to death, but the thought did not occur to her, accustomed as she was to my talking from another world – and being very much alive! She asked the nurse what drugs he was having and learned that he was still having Largactil, but this was being doubled up with haloperidol. This was a drug I had frequently been given on hospital admissions.

In due course Alex was given forty-eight hours' leave, with instructions to return on Monday. The leave was wonderful, but the return haunted him. Mum assured him that this was just a formality. I had always been released like that. They just wanted to check up and make sure everyone was happy. He didn't believe her. He was sure they had some Machiavellian plan to keep him in and it scared him stiff. He was right; he was expected to stay the night, at least. The doctor had not yet arrived. Mum asked if she might speak to him. They were allowed to sit in the open ward, through which the doctor was expected to pass, with his retinue, on their way to the committee room.

The doctor's party came into sight, in close formation, and walked towards them. As they approached, Mum rose to speak to the great man. He did not appear to have seen her. The procession passed on, untroubled. They had reached the safety of their door before Mum regained her breath.

"I'll come in with you when you are called," she said to Alex, to his immense comfort.

A few minutes later they were ushered into the presence. Mum didn't know what to expect, having already written to the great man, without reply, but they were greeted courteously.

"I understand that you want Alex to come in regularly for injections? And that he is very reluctant to have them?"

"That is far the most sensible course of treatment. If he goes on like this, his life won't be worth living. He'll become a cabbage."

Mum retorted: "Is it fair to talk about 'going on like this'? He would not be here now if we had not all let him down. He managed to stay away for six months, which surprised everyone here. Then the pressure did get too great and he came back. But he should not have had to come back *again*, only you overprescribed for him, and no one would authorise a reduction, and when he knew he had to return, though it was the very *last* thing he wanted to do, he found he could not get in!"

"Well, of course that is why it is so much better to treat these sort of patients on a regular basis, so that these crises don't arise. After all, there are times when we are very short-staffed and cannot deal with situations other than routine. The staff have to go off duty sometimes, you know."

"In that case, if you are all on holiday," Mum was incensed, "I'll give him the injection myself, if that is necessary."

The great man laughed, the woman was absurd.

"I could," she said, indignantly, "I'm a nurse."

"It would be most unsuitable. You wouldn't like to do it."

"No, I certainly wouldn't. But if he needed it and there was nobody else to do it, I would. Though actually, if he were treated in time, he wouldn't need an injection. What other drugs do you give him that I could give him at home?"

"I can't prescribe for him to be treated at home, under those circumstances. It would be too dangerous."

Mum remembered seeing Alex at death's door, and believed him.

"Can anyone else prescribe for him?"

"Oh yes, Dr Arkwright is your doctor. He can prescribe for him."

"Good. Thank you very much. That's all we need to know." She smiled happily, rose, and signaled to Alex.

"Goodbye."

"Goodbye, and good luck."

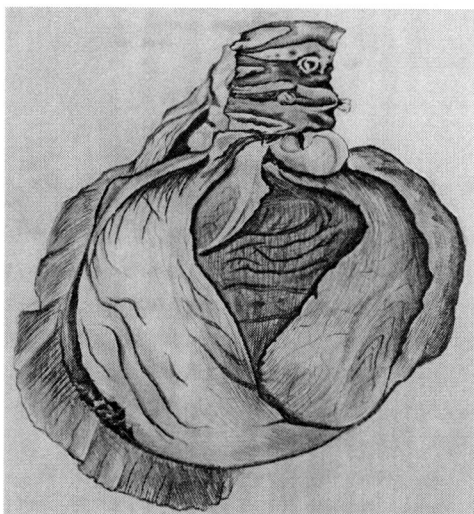

Chapter 16

McDonald's

A psychiatric prescription must be an onerous responsibility, especially for a GP, who is not a specialist. But Mum was only concerned for Alex's health and if she could guide the GP, it would then largely be her own responsibility. She was quite prepared for that. They went together to see Dr Arkwright and explain the position. He trusted them and prescribed haloperidol to be kept in reserve. In the meantime, Alex was to continue reporting to the clinic, as before. This meant queuing up to see a doctor who knew little about him, and cared less, according to Alex. This was hardly fair of him, but one must expect an ex-patient, who has been seen only as a down-and-out, to feel bitter.

An appointment was made for him, which was later changed.

"If they can't make up their minds when they want to see me, I shan't bother to go at all." Alex was feeling better. Five years later, he has not been near the place since. During those five years he has learned to establish his independence. Fate has provided him with a programme of ever-increasing challenges, so that his self-respect and self-confidence are fully restored, and there is no lurking fear of a return to the bad old days. With Les's help, I too kept free of hospital. His regimen for me was: regular highly nutritious meals; two hours exercise daily, to promote sleep; the Alexander Technique and early to bed. He himself only needed two hours sleep a night and was habitually studying seven profound books.

Alex reduced his dosage, sensibly, gradually over the next two months. Christmas was the first challenge. It had never felt right since Father died, and last year it had been particularly traumatic with Alex behaving like an ancient prophet proclaiming doom: not a memory anyone wanted to associate with Christmas. The occasion passed without mishap.

He received a Christmas card from one of his old friends at the hospital where he had worked in Sussex. He'd not been in touch with any of them since he left two years before. Marie now proposed to come and see him. She would be staying with her mother nearby.

This was an even bigger challenge. His secret was safe from all his friends. They knew nothing of his breakdown. And he wanted to keep it that way. He liked to remember his happy days there as the life and soul of the night staff. Though only the night porter, he was often mistaken for a doctor and always included in the nurses' parties. He was much admired as an artist. His gentle but commanding presence, his readiness to joke, and his diplomacy made him a sought after friend. He corresponded with nurses all over the world when they returned to their own countries. He had left with a testimonial, which he was tempted to keep in the bank. Happy days indeed! He did not want to spoil that image. He had never been in love with Marie. They were close friends; but she was a girl, and sexual feelings were especially vulnerable in time of mental stress. It was a challenge. He had been unused to any social life, other than family and Stan and Elsie with her teapot.

She arrived a couple of days after Christmas. He was feeling quite strong and was pleased to see her. She brought a pot of three colourful polyanthus plants, which brightened the house and would become the very first garden plants. The day was most enjoyable. Mum had prepared lunch and afterwards the two went out to walk over the hill and talk about old times. Two years was a long stretch. They came in hungry for tea and sat by the fire, which Alex had lit earlier. Mum noted anxiously that they both seemed happy, *normal*, whatever that might be?

Suddenly, Alex, saying something rather peevish, rushed out of the room. Marie was taken by surprise, but Mum realised that he had managed to keep a "good face" for just so long, but had come to the end of his tether. She handed Marie a piece of cake, wondering how much she could explain before Alex came back.

"I'm so sorry," she said. "I know he didn't mean to be rude, but he has been very ill since you knew him, and he is not fully recovered. He's doing awfully well and he was so pleased to see you. But it has been a bit much. We hardly see anyone here."

"We hadn't heard anything of him for such a long time. We wondered why not."

"Well, that's why." Mum smiled ruefully. "I'm afraid I must ask you to go now, if you've finished your tea? I really am sorry." And she hustled the bemused girl out to her car. There was no sign of Alex.

"The interfering old battle-axe! I feel as if I had been frog-marched!" Marie was indignant. "She's got him at last. I know she's been trying long enough. Wait till I tell the girls!"

Alex emerged after she had gone, chagrined to have let himself down. It had been a wonderful day, but just a bit too long for a first effort at sociability. Mum wrote and made peace with Marie who wrote a charming, understanding letter in reply, promising to come again when Alex was feeling better. Alex, who was off his pills, took one that evening, slept well, and returned to normal for the next few weeks.

As April approached, Mum became uncomfortably conscious that the new rates were looming and that her unfinished cottage, having furniture in it was going to attract a hefty bill. It must be emptied. She asked Donald to go up with his van and rescue a number of boxes. She was going to have to cut her losses and let the furniture go to auction. She would, however, have to go up there to arrange for a sale.

Alex saw how her mind was working. It worried him. He did not want to go back to the scene of his horror. Nor did he feel like being left on his own. He went to visit a friend to whom he had sold his original terrace property. It happened that Tom was about to go away, leaving a cat and telephone unattended. Alex saw his chance. He could not go north if he were manning the telephone and the cat needed feeding. He volunteered for duty and was gratefully accepted.

Tom was to bring the key over with final instructions when he finished work. Six or seven o'clock, they thought, but it was nearer half past nine when he came, and he had come for the evening. Alex usually went to bed at ten, and he liked time to unwind before going up. He was already slightly disturbed when Tom's van refused to start. After the usual bonnet searching he pushed the vehicle down the lane. By this time he was very wide-awake. They went together next morning to open up shop and feed the cat. Alex took himself off for a walk while Mum settled with the cat by the silent telephone. Alex came back at lunchtime and they drank their soup and ate their sandwiches. Alex had had a splendid time looking up old friends round Colne, but Mum could not think that either of them was doing anything of vital importance. They agreed to go home and return next morning to feed the cat. They kept it up all week, but Alex was obviously unsettled, and, from what he told her, he must have been leaving some puzzled people behind, and some raised eyebrows.

"Alex, you're getting too high. You really do need to take your pills again," she said on more than one occasion.

"I'm perfectly all right. I never felt better in my life. *I* know when I need to take a pill."

But of course, that was the whole point! He didn't. The better he felt, at this stage, the more he was in need, and the less likely to see it. He began to get cross when she mentioned it, so, worried out of her wits, she stopped mentioning it, praying for the week to end, when they could stay quietly at home. But before that, came the memorable Saturday.

Alex suggested going to the pub. He never drank, but Mum encouraged him, when he felt fit, to go for a game of snooker, or simply to meet people. This time a man was already propping up the bar. He seemed interested in Alex, and asked him questions, trying to place him. When high, natural diffidence is left behind. Alex parried his questions with some very pertinent ones of his own, which he would not have dreamed of doing normally. It was all highly entertaining and Mum forgot her anxiety in her pride to see him holding his own so well.

"Look here," the man laughed good-naturedly. "I'm the one asking the questions. It's my job: I'm a policeman! Who are you, anyway? Are you Bernard Ingram?"

That made Alex's day. But he wanted to move on.

"Let's go to McDonald's!"

They had often been there for their supper when he took her to the pictures on a weekday. There were not many people there as a rule. But this was Saturday and it was crowded. The place seemed to be teeming with teenagers, all there to enjoy themselves. Alex spotted a pretty girl and couldn't take his eyes off her.

Oh dear! Trouble, thought Mum, as she tried to head him away. She managed to get him, reluctantly, outside, but when she tried to turn left, with the idea of going back to the car, he would have none of it. They walked round the shopping precinct, passing a pair of policewomen. Mum wondered if they noticed anything. Might she need to call them back? All went well until their circular tour brought them back to the McDonald's entrance. As luck would have it, the gang, in their tee shirts, was just coming out.

"You go back to the car, Mother," he said grimly, giving her a little push and crossing the road to join the gang.

She decided that it would not be a good moment for her to rejoin him; better to keep a distant eye on him walking parallel on the opposite side of the road.

"You want to take him home, missus," one of the lads called to her.

"That's exactly what I'm trying to do," she called back. "But it's easier said than done."

Eventually, she was able to catch up with Alex and take him across the road away from the crowd. He had simmered down by then, but was dishevelled. She helped him tidy up and as she did so, a young lad came across to them carrying his tie.

"He left this behind."

Mum thanked him. She was touched by his courage, as much as by his courtesy. Alex was oblivious. He was a spent force and ready for home. The penny seemed to have dropped at last and when she told him she simply could not keep him out of hospital if he did not take his pills, he was ready to believe her. He took two that night and slept, but was still restless.

She gave him two more in the morning at about eight o'clock. They had no effect, so she gave him another at half past ten. Dangerous drugs should not be given at less than four hourly intervals. Mum didn't like it, but if there was no effect...? And there was still no effect. Two more at one o'clock. One more at three o'clock and still no effect, but at least Alex was co-operating. At six o'clock she gave him yet two more, and each time, the Orphenadrine needed to counteract side effects. Now, at long last, after another hour, having taken a monumental dose of eight hundred grams of Largactil in ten hours, Alex began to respond. His restlessness left him and he was able to relax. He did not fall asleep, but he was ready for bed when the time came. She gave him two more, to make sure, and he slept like a baby. (This do-it-yourself treatment is not recommended, but it worked this time. There is no doubt that it is dangerous.)

The next morning the release from anxiety was so great for both of them that they felt like new. It really seemed that Alex had routed his demon completely. He was chirpy and clear-headed as a bell. He asked if he might walk into town. It was a beautiful day, why not? It was Sunday morning. Mum might as well have her bath as usual, while he was out. She ran the bath and got in. The phone rang. Panic! What could have happened? She raced downstairs clutching a towel.

"Is that Mrs Dalglish? Alex has just been in. He asked me to ring and let you know that he's on his way to town and that he's quite all right."

That was the kind people who had once entertained them to tea. She smiled. Bless him! He must have a guilty conscience about the dance he had led her all week.

She went back to her bath, well content, stepped into it and stretched out, wallowing. The phone rang again. She dripped her way down again, not quite so fast.

"Is that Mrs Dalglish?"

"It is."

"Alex has just been in and he asked me…"

The next farm down the road. And again. But who cares about the lingering luxury of a bath, when all these people were ready to rejoice with her? And with such cause for rejoicing.

The astonishing thing is that Alex never took any more Largactil from that day, with a few occasional exceptions. But that is the whole art: to know when to take them, and to take them in time. It is the strongest possible argument for the adage, "a stitch in time saves nine". It is not easy to recognise the necessity, but well worth learning the art.

Chapter 17

Gardens

The next three years passed, for Alex and for me, without mishap. I kept in touch with Dr Bob and the clinic. I took lithium carbonate and had a regular blood count test. Alex refused to take anything at all but kept medication handy in case of emergency. For a long time intensive care had been needed – not the hospital interpretation of the term – but intensive nonetheless. Strict vigilance would always be needed, but his tolerance level gradually improved. At one time he found the slightest sounds unbearable: the burble of the oil-fired Aga, Mum eating toast, a door rattling was enough to worry him. As for the mixer or the washing machine, they drove him straight out of the room. Now the Aga was acceptable; Mum was allowed to eat her toast, and none of the doors dared to rattle since he had dealt with them. The other essential noises Mum timed to match his absence. In time these too became acceptable. The utter peace of their surroundings and the succession of small amounts of containable stress, which life inevitably throws up, formed the background of his recovery. It was as if there was an ordained programme for recovery. Each small triumph was followed by a tougher test. With each he gained in confidence and courage.

Les and I enjoyed his visits with Mum because he was getting back to his chatty self, the old Alex, who could make us all laugh with his jokes. Where did he get them all from? Maybe back numbers of the *Readers' Digest*, but his memory was sharp and he was good at punch lines. Les was a natural wit and could introduce any topic under the sun for discussion. We all compared notes and learned a great deal about our predicament.

Although there were many days when Les and I walked together up the hills, along the lanes and through the woods, I found my greatest fulfilment glorifying his garden. Les was very proud, not only of my gardening prowess, but my ability to unravel the mysteries of the word processor, which his family had given him to write the books he had in mind. In fact, every time we had written a million words he would say: "Delete," to my horror. He had been a newspaper editor at one stage, and words were expendable. My husband had tried to teach me non-attachment when it came to family furniture and materials. Les was teaching me a new sort of non-attachment.

Lucky, the little black and white cat that had come to live with Mum and me at John Peel's cottage, so diffidently, now lived with us in Friar Row. No one knew *her* age or sex, but she didn't make an issue of it and remained the soul of discretion, the perfect pet. How often had she lain lightly on my sternum looking into my eyes while I lay down to do my Alexander Technique?

One thing worried Les. What would happen to me when he died? The bungalow we lived in belonged to his family. He had always been freelance and lived now only on a state pension. I had no capital, apart from the remains of the marital home, and my income was the Independent Carer's Allowance. Mum, having sold one of her Ruthwaite cottages, came to my rescue and made it possible for me to buy a downstairs flat with a neglected garden a few hundred yards from Les's bungalow. Renovating the flat absorbed much of my boundless energy and gave me a new purpose in life, a new root. Together Les and I cleared the nettles from the back. We built in steps and a rockery. Les made a wooden Rose arch. I planted fragrant roses and together we barrowed away the buttercups and laid a heart-shaped lawn with gravel path. We gave it to Holiday Home letting agents who let it for nine months of the year.

At the same time Alex thought of renting Higher Clough to holidaymakers to provide him with an income without the stress and odium of seeking employment. But where would he and Mum go meanwhile? Another idea he had entertained, as a source of income: no one would employ him as an unqualified tradesman, but he could do a pretty good job as builder, joiner, plumber, electrician, plasterer and tiler. Higher Clough would be valuable collateral if he were to borrow from the bank in order to buy a terraced house. If he managed to buy at the right price and work on a neglected property, he could put his skills to good use and sell at a profit. Why not combine the two ideas?

He found the ideal property, in a quiet street with a front garden bordering an open space to the south: a suntrap, a passing neighbour assured them. That was enough for Mum. She could live happily there for the summer. Alex too was thrilled. They had been very lucky to find this place. It needed little doing to it and should give a profitable interest. Alex put the matter into the hands of a lawyer and they turned their interest to Higher Clough once more.

The holiday agent who came out to inspect was encouraging, promising to put details in the next brochure. They discussed terms. Mum felt herself to be more experienced than Alex.

"For pity's sake, don't put us in too high a grade!" she said. "One agent gave me the benefit of the doubt once and graded my property higher than it warranted. Some of my visitors seemed to expect a sauna or something. I don't know which of us was more indignant!"

"That can be embarrassing," the agent smiled.

"I do like visitors to be happy when they come; though some of them never will be, no matter how hard you try. They seem to bring their unhappiness with them. Though I must say, most people are very nice and friendly."

Terms were agreed, and the charming agent, who seemed to love their setting, took her leave. They had given her tea by the new window upstairs. The view was stunning.

The contract was signed for the terraced house. Alex could begin work there as soon as he liked. The brochure arrived with a most attractive write-up and sketch of Higher Clough.

"It's as big as a telephone directory!" said Alex, impressed. "How on earth are people going to pick us out of all that lot?"

"We may not be booked every week," Mum warned. "I think they reckon to let for twenty weeks in the season, but we don't want to open too soon, and we want to get back before the central heating is necessary, so we may not do too well. But anyway, we can sneak back when it is not let."

"That would enable us to clean up better before the next visitors. I don't know how we are going to get the job done if someone else is coming in the same day."

"It's a bit of a scramble at the best of times, and I doubt it would reach your standard of perfection. But visitors are supposed to leave the place, as they would like to find it. Their standards vary of course. Some are jolly good, but as old Bill used to say, 'The best visitors are the ones that pay and don't come.'"

The garden became important. It hardly existed as yet, but the dream was there and the first steps had been taken. Last year Mum, who had been impatient to this end ever since Alex bought the place ten years earlier, had asked the farmer to deliver a load of muck. She had returned one day with the shopping and found that he had not only delivered it but kindly spread the load all over the triangle of stone-heaped clay. It was a start, but being two feet deep and fresh, it was unattractive as a working medium. However, time had worked wonders. The top had dried and could be scraped off and removed to do good elsewhere, while the base could be raked clear of stones, forked over, and potatoes planted. As the potatoes were lifted, the resulting soil was good enough for anything – better at least than

144

any other patch in the garden. It seemed to be fairly sheltered too, thus providing a starting place for many treasures.

When Alex had bought Higher Clough, no thought of a garden had entered his head. Even Mum could scarcely imagine landscaping so difficult a site. The cart track led from the lane to the north of the farmhouse, up beside the beck to the west, and beyond the house to the south, turning back down the hill and through two gates to the farmyard and front door on the southern side. The south front was built close into the hill and had a claustrophobic air. In early days Alex saw the merits of having the entrance to the north. It would save a great deal of drive making, when such a thing had to be made. It would leave the south side potentially clear. Funds, at the time, stretched to the making of a new entrance and limited reinforcement to the cart track. Later operations had gravelled a turning space in front of the house and shifted hundreds of tons of earth from the south front together with a quantity of stone and rubble resulting from the demolished byre. But it was never clearly defined where this was to go to: there really was nowhere for it to go to at all. It had been piled high in that area designated "kitchen garden", and lay, dutifully flat, but level with the *top* of the surrounding wall; sufficiently high in a valley to catch all the wind. And still they could do with pushing a bit more soil away from the house.

It was no good planting like that. They must get rid of a vast amount; even if it meant paying lorries to take it away. On their budget, that was a depressing thought. Instead, they asked the farmer if they could tip it over the wall, in a hollow, towards the beck.

"I couldn't let you do that! A storm might wash that lot into the beck and fill it up. Then it might stop the water getting through to the rest of the stock. I might let you put it further down the lane."

But that would mean the expense of lorries anyway, or running the JCB up and down the lane forever and a day

145

with tiny loads. There was another possibility: the land beyond their southeast boundary dipped before it rose sharply in a little gully. This was nearly always dry but became torrential after a storm. Mum had once cast covetous eyes on it on Alex's behalf, as a potential garden feature. But no farmer sells the smallest piece of possible grazing, so she had given up hope. Could they now use this dip as a dumping ground? The grass would grow again, no doubt.

The farmer considered. He didn't like putting a spanner in their works. They were no trouble to him as neighbours; they'd even let him know once when a cow had calved unexpectedly. Farming was in a bad way: a little ready cash might not come amiss.

"I don't fancy having so much rubbish tipped on my land," he said, "and you'll have an awful lot no doubt? But I might consider selling you that bit with the gully."

Mum could hardly contain her joy. But such joy is expensive and they were going to have to find the money somehow for the lorries if it had come to that. Perhaps the land would cost no more? It could not be worth very much as grazing? If only the farmer would really let them have it! Finally, they agreed a price and the JCB moved in.

This time, the results were breathtaking. Alex and Mum revelled in walking around their new shaped acre, deciding just where each section of the garden should be and from which spots the best views were to be seen, for here there would be seats made, of course, by Alex. The vegetable patch, lying comfortably within its protecting walls, was overlooked by the potential summerhouse, from where would be the most spectacular view of all. The new feature, a pond would also be seen from the summerhouse, and in between, would be the shrubbery on one side, a sweeping path down to the house bordering a mighty bank of heathers and azaleas. Only dwarf azaleas, of course, or you would not see the shrubbery from the house.

The JCB had cut the pipe that used to bring water from the spring to the farmyard and to the single tap in the old scullery. Alex traced the pipe back and directed the flow into the newly formed pond outside the sitting room window. Here they dreamed of water lilies. Another beneficial mishap was when the JCB, lowering the level of the kitchen garden, went too bravely near the edge, over the wall built by Donald in Alex's absence. The wall crumbled into the path, but the skill of the driver saved himself and the machine. This reproach remained for some months until Alex suddenly realised that the only way up to the vegetable garden was right round the house. Mum could see them going without vegetables when the weather was bad, if she had the fetching of them.

The break in the wall was obviously the ideal place for steps. Alex bought a load of paving stones from a demolition site. There was no room for them in the narrow passage, so each one, weighing two to four hundredweight, had to be man-handled from the drop to the site. The first one buckled the trolley, so each had to be *walked* along to its position and, after the first, lifted, single-handed. Mum knew that she could help best by keeping out of the way. Two or three stones were enough for one day, with easier jobs in between; but the task was completed. The creation of the garden was absorbing. They almost forgot about the terrace house and the need to clear out of Higher Clough for holidaymakers.

"We're never going to be ready for visitors!" Mum exclaimed one day.

"Do you think they would mind us working in the garden while they're here?" Alex asked, hopefully.

"I shouldn't think they'd like it very much! I shouldn't like the owner checking up on me if I were staying."

"How are we going to keep pace with things in the garden if we have to be away all summer?"

"And how are we going to get the house ready if we don't start now?"

"We can't do it, can we?"

"Do you think we could possibly back out at this late stage?"

"We can't leave them in the lurch. But I must say, the thought of living in that poky little town house, when we could be living here, doesn't appeal very much. I wonder if they have taken any bookings for us. We haven't heard. Let's give them a ring."

They were in luck. No firm bookings had been taken, though there had been one or two enquiries. It was disappointing, but not unduly inconvenient. The agent was charming as ever and promised to put them back on their lists should circumstances change. What a relief!

Chapter 18

Dandan's Centenary

Things were going so well that there really seemed to be no longer any excuse for not going to see Dandan. She had settled in remarkably well in the residential home to which Bim had taken her in Sussex. He had found it, newly opened, close to her old home and she had been able to choose her room and generally organise the place to her liking. Mum had heard from Theresa that there was a verandah the whole length of the southern side, part of which was enclosed to make a suntrap. This Dandan had commandeered for her own use. She was doing very nicely, thank you: a born survivor.

Mum had long absolved her conscience on Dandan's score. She was far better off living in a grand house in the style to which she was accustomed. It was a long journey, three hundred miles, and a long time since she or Alex had driven so far. They would have to stay a night or two, but it was time they were a bit more adventurous. The idea of staying away from home, away from their accustomed anchor of security was itself alarming. Suppose Alex should panic? It was an awful long way from home. Suppose he should find the journey too long? It would be an affront to his masculinity if she were to drive. He'd never be able to sleep in a strange bed. He'd be worn out, and you know what two sleepless nights can do. And then he'd have the journey home. Stop fussing, Mother, he's got to start sometime.

Theresa, Dandan's friend, to whom Mum had been writing, offered to put them up. This made everything as easy as possible. If anyone understood the situation, she did. Theresa was accustomed to awkward people, and nothing would offend her. She had a great admiration of Dandan and was pleased to help her family revisit her.

The length of the journey still worried Mum, until she remembered Carol's mother, Grace, who lived halfway between them and their ultimate destination. If they were to take her out to lunch one day and manage that return journey safely, they could face the trip south with confidence. They travelled on a Sunday to avoid heavy traffic. Even so, there was more than there used to be, but Alex was not unduly harassed. In Sussex they found themselves passing through the village where they had first lived after the divorce. The car came to an unexpected halt. They were just outside the Garage where Mum had once held an account. She still remembered the feeling of quicksand when the bills came in: Charles, the only other car-borne member of the family, sharing the source of petrol.

Being Sunday, the Garage was closed, but there was a telephone next door so Mum phoned Theresa.

"It's strange that you should ring. I've just been having a nap and I had a feeling that you would! Yes, of course I'll come and fetch you. I may be about half an hour."

They waited happily in the old familiar terrain. If one had to have a breakdown one could hardly do it more comfortably. Theresa's superb hospitality began a little early but remained superb throughout their visit. She had prepared some delicious meals, which were a lovely change from their usual rather Spartan diet, and about which she was unjustifiably modest. She lit the wood fire in the sitting room and the central heating was in full use – all very comfortable. And what is more, she offered them the use of her own car while they were there in case they wanted to see old friends in different directions. What a truly thoughtful and generous hostess!

It was lovely to see her again and get to know her better. Though Mum had been corresponding with her since she first took Dandan up to John Peel's cottage, and Dandan would not do her own writing, they had not previously been friends. Mum never fraternised with Dandan's friends, knowing that their total allegiance was hers, and that she must rather distrust them or disillusion them. She doubted whether she could do this and didn't bother to try. But Theresa was different. She realised the truth, while sympathising with both.

Dandan looked marvellous! Mum had not seen her since abandoning her in that distant rest home, two whole years ago in 1985. And here she was, having had a bath, her white hair beautifully brushed and fastened at the top of her head in a minute bun. (Even in her younger days it had been rudely referred to as a "currant", but she would never have it cut.) She looked radiant, her eyes as blue as ever. But she was in bed. The nurse explained as she showed Mum into her room, "She's a little tired this morning. She's normally up and about."

This didn't sound like the Dandan Mum remembered. Dandan tired? She was indefatigable. Had she really lost so much ground? Mum felt a pang. But as soon as she saw her she realised what it was all about. Dandan had been given a bath in her honour. She was not tired. She was furious. Still the consummate actress, she would not admit defeat, but would protest in the only way available to her. They had exhausted her with their barbaric treatment, just when she should have been at her best. What sort of nurses did they think themselves?

"I'm sorry to find you in bed. I'd hoped to take you out to lunch."

"Oh how lovely!"

"Nurse says you are too tired. I must say: you don't look it!"

"I'm not tired."

"Do you think you could manage lunch?"

"Of course I could."

"Shall I call the nurse to help you dress?"

"You can help me, can't you?" Dandan climbed nimbly out of bed.

"Of course I can. Where are your clothes?"

Mum would never have been allowed to help in the old days. Could Dandan be mellowing?

They found a parking space where there was none (special concession for age) outside their favourite restaurant where Dandan proved that her appetite was unabated. It was something of a joke that, when she was taken out to lunch, she would be undefeated by a man-size portion, tiny as she was.

After lunch they drove round the old haunts, Dandan enjoying the change of scene; Mum remembering the bitterness with which these haunts were drenched, thankful that time had dealt kindly with her bitterness. Later they returned to the home, where tea was served in Dandan's private suntrap; but not before Mum had been shown round and shown off. Visitors were used as counters on a scoreboard, according to gender, relationship and frequency. Dandan's standing was good, in that she had a devoted son who visited regularly, scoring top marks. But it was known that she had a daughter who, though less valuable on the scoreboard, was nevertheless something of an indictment by her absence. Here, at last, was vindication.

One of the old ladies caught hold of Mum.

"What a wonderful old lady your mother is! She is so *sweet*! Has she always been as sweet as this?" Innocently.

Mum was spared the embarrassment of an answer by Dandan's impatience for tea. She reported the incident to Theresa who laughed.

"Your mother is a great many things, but I don't think I would have said that sweetness was one of them."

Alex too visited Dandan, a great excitement for the old ladies. With those looks, how had he managed to stay single all these years? Top score, without a doubt. Alex also went in the evening to see some old friends, including Marie. It was quite a challenge but he had made headway since Marie had come to see him at Higher Clough, and it was good to see them all again and to hold his own with them. That night he hardly slept, but that was to be expected. The next day they took quietly, walking and talking with Theresa, Mum paying Dandan a brief visit, resting before the rigours of the return journey. Alex decided to take a Largactil pill to be on the safe side. Mum was delighted to see him come to this decision unaided. She could feel confident now, that he could recognise his dangers and take steps to avoid them. That was more than half the battle. This journey would have been worthwhile if only on that account. It was good to know that the old hostilities were dead between herself and Dandan: another milestone passed. They returned happily to their tranquil haven.

As the weeks went by, Mum kept hoping for a full return to normal in Alex's health. Surely he must get back to full strength, without those bouts of fatigue, headache and woolly heads? They were obviously genuine. Alex was no actor, nor malingerer. And after all, he was not expected by the medical profession to be able to manage at all without everlasting pills and/or injections and/or return visits to hospital. Mum should not expect too much. But she did. And it worried her.

It occurred to her that she and Alex had not been out of each other's sight for more than a few hours since they returned to Higher Clough. Alex was gaining steadily in confidence, but Mum had reached a point where her gastric ulcer, ever a barometer to her own health, was now reacting to Alex's condition. If his mood sank she had to take a stomach powder. This was ridiculous! It must be time for a break. In any case, it would be another step in his recovery, to be more independent of her.

Simon invited Alex to stay with him. Enough water had passed under the bridge since that catastrophic visit for them both to be ready to renew a very real, lifelong friendship. Mum went to her old friend and cousin near Salisbury. He lived an idyllic bachelor life surrounded by charming widows, all of whom thought him incapable of looking after himself and all eager to oblige. He was, in fact, extremely capable and had no intention at all of succumbing. Dear Robert! He had often stayed with Mum before she became so involved with Dandan and me.

He had not changed. The smile with which he greeted her spread and wrinkled his whole face, just as it had done when she was a child. She remembered how, as a big cousin, he had *found* her Saturday penny. Funny how it had come to be in his pocket. He had always been kind to her. When she had announced her engagement to Peter Dalglish, Robert had written to remind her that she had once asked *him* to marry her. She had forgotten but told him that if the answer had been yes, he'd left it twenty years too long.

It was now "happy hour" as soon as she settled in. Tea did not feature very largely in his routine. He offered her whisky, which she never drank, but rules are made to be broken. All the anxieties and frustrations of the last few years and of the recent drive soon rolled away in utter relaxation. She was no longer the strong man of the party, the tower of strength. He would take the weight off her feet as it were. It was bliss. It was luxury beyond her remembrance. She could talk without having to be careful. She could tell him everything without fear of his disapproval, horror even. He must have been shocked by some of the things she told him. Misunderstanding is only to be expected in a subject on which most people are ignorant. But if he did not fully understand, he gave no hint of criticism, and the spate of her revelation left her somehow exorcised.

It was a wonderfully recuperative week spent exchanging "happy hours" with his merry widows and other friends. They took a picnic one day to a local beauty spot, and another day they went to visit Dandan. He had always been fond of her and amused by the warfare between Mum and his aunt. Dandan was delighted to see them. Mum had not given warning of their coming so that she did not have to be subjected to the indignity of a bath.

"You look like Robert Schuster," she said, her blue eyes radiant as ever.

"I *am* Robert Schuster. How nice to see you!" His face crinkled once more as he chuckled in amusement. But Dandan had already dismissed him.

"Doesn't he look like Robert Schuster, Moll?"

"He should do! He really is, you know!"

But Dandan was not convinced or even any longer interested. He was a visitor and as such should be entertained as was fitting. She chatted socially, a gift that Mum had always envied her, of this and that. Her stock was limited and her memory not all that it had been, but she brought freshness to each repeated gambit. When it was time for them to go, she offered them the amenities of the house. It was a superb performance.

"She *is* a remarkable old lady!" he chuckled as they left. His admiration for her had been genuine since the days when he was staying with Mum. Dandan, still driving in her eighties, had insisted on taking him to church, taking his life in her hands, with scant regard to his wishes or his nerves.

Mum wanted to see a married cousin with whom she had been to school. They had much in common, having matching mothers. Aunt Mary had lived to be ninety-six, Dandan was still going strong. She invited herself to lunch. She set off early, not knowing the road or studying it and found herself already there, an hour too soon. In her timeless tranquility back home she had forgotten the value of punctuality and rang the bell an hour early.

It was a mistake. Her cousins had a tight schedule. He had retired from military command. They had been shopping and arrived back as she came in sight. There was lunch still to prepare. And here was another scatterbrained member of the family. Such irresponsibility was too bad. They did their best to make her welcome and she enjoyed herself no end, but the floodgate had already been opened and the spate continued.

Suddenly it was halted.

155

"Stop. Don't say another word!" He pushed a magazine in her hands saying, "Read that. And don't say anything."

Drastic action? There was no doubt about it: Mum had been talking far too much and far too fast. So this was what it was like from the other side of the fence when she realised that first I, then Simon, then Alex was in danger of going too far. It was all right for Mum: there was nothing in her history that would suggest that she was going out of her mind, but perhaps it could happen.

She left soon after and asked Robert that evening, "Do you think I've gone round the bend?"

He looked vague, unconcerned: "Certainly not! Why do you ask?"

"I just wondered." She was reassured and laughingly told him of the consternation she had caused. His apparent unconcern comforted her. Fear begets fear and he showed none of it. Later, he confessed that he had been worried himself.

Simon and Alex had enjoyed their break and, visits over, they returned home in good spirits. It was another milestone happily passed. The next one on the calendar was Dandan's century: 19th November 1987. It seemed strange to Mum that after so many years of attendance she would have nothing to do with the organising of this event, but Bim and Stella, who had been looking after her, had arranged with the proprietor for a suitable celebration. All Mum had to do was put in an appearance.

There were further implications in the occasion. It was deemed a good enough excuse for Charles to bring his whole family from Australia: a great opportunity for them to meet their English cousins, as well as pay homage to a memorable forebear. Our great grandmother's hundredth birthday, and we were there. What a proud boast back home! Charles closed his business early enough for Christmas to take in the birthday, which gave them over a month.

Mum, the old mother hen, hoped that they would make their headquarters at Higher Clough. Alex, a realist, was not so sure. How could they all adapt to their very different ways of life? Theirs at Higher Clough was practically still life, whereas the Aussies were all accustomed to working hard and playing hard. How could Mum cater for them all when she was only used to their own meager appetites? And, most of all, how were they going to keep the Australians warm in mid-winter?

"Don't fuss so much," Mum said. "We've got central heating haven't we, even if we don't ever use it? Now is our chance to try it out. And if you think I can't feed them all, how do you think I brought you lot up at the farm?"

These were not his only worries. The sitting room was in a dreadful state: the walls still damp, plaster coming off, mould. They couldn't sit in it even with the central heating and the wood fire. And the carpet! Too small, the wrong colour and, being unloved, full of holes from escaping embers. Alex could not hold his head up as the owner of such a room, especially as host to big brother, Charles, the tycoon, with whom, as youngest, he had always been at a disadvantage.

There was only one thing for it. Charles and his family were coming so Alex must tackle the sitting room. They had plenty of warning so that the task could be done at leisure. Alex liked to take his time over everything and do it all to perfection. It would have been hopeless to hustle him. As it was he made an excellent job. They were able to find a new carpet of which he fully approved. The results gave them both huge satisfaction and he began to look forward to the visit with enthusiasm. He took his paintings out of their portfolio for the first time since that awful day when they arrived back from the hospital to live here together; when he had looked at his house and his pictures and believed them to be a total loss, like his own life, without hope of recovery. Two years it had taken, but hope was surely rekindled? One day he would paint again!

He rescued several pastels, looking at them critically.

"Do you know, these are not so bad, after all? I think that one is even quite good! We need some more pictures to go on the sitting room wall."

Mum never knew quite what to say about his pictures. She was no artist and she had learned that criticism, even when invited, was not required: being uninformed it was unhelpful and could be destructive. She just felt in her bones that he had it in him to be an artist and that one day he would fulfil his potential. Even if she were wrong, he'd done well, surely?

Alex busied himself now with framing the best of his finds ready for the sitting room wall. Two portraits demanded a matching pair of oval mountings: a tricky operation. He had once watched an expert, wasting sheets of card in abortive effort. But he had a tool and he wanted to try it. His self-esteem rose even higher as he turned out two perfect oval mountings, without waste. He hung his pictures, arranging them carefully on the walls: portraits in the dining room; landscapes in the sitting room; abstracts in his bedroom, others elsewhere.

Now he could face the visitors. And now it was time to prepare for the *birthday*. Theresa was going to put them up again. Simon had his own friends nearby and some other friends of Dandan's who were accustomed to Heathrow's early hours offered to meet and accommodate Charles's family. The first that Mum and Alex would see of them would be at the party. This was another ordeal for Alex. In his working days he had been the life and soul at hospital parties, quick-witted and good fun; but this was family. They all knew about him and none of them would understand. He expected to be looked upon as something from outer space. In fact, they were all pleased to see him looking so well.

Bim and Stella were a sociable couple and gathered all concerned for the occasion and notified others who should register, so that there was a good showing of telegrams, including the one from the Queen, one from Dandan's MP, one from her original Mothers' Union (known irreverently by her family as Mother's onion), and one from the cricket club at Mobberley. Her entitlement to this was through her husband who, like everyone else in the village good for five guineas, was vice-president for life.

It was a proud day for the proprietress. It was not every home that could boast a centenarian and such a sprightly one. They were all pleased to take part in such a celebration and apart from the inevitable champagne, Mrs Armitage had taken pains to provide delicacies, many of which she had made herself, with great professionalism.

Dandan was seated centre stage where everyone had a chance to speak with her. To her right was seated her old gardener, whom Alex had collected from a nearby home. He had been a faithful old friend, known to most of them: this was a day he would remember. Alex was glad of the excuse to make himself scarce.

Mum paid her respects, and turned her attention to her Australian family. She had seen Charles at Simon's party and Carol when she came on her own, but she had not set eyes on her grandchildren since she last went to Australia four years before. They had been children then. Now, at seventeen, Faye was a beautiful young woman and, though only fifteen, Robert, in his brand new suit, was almost a man. Dandan, alas, had no idea who they were. This was a tremendous day for her. She had been looking forward to it for months, asking Bim each time he came, "Have I missed it?"

"No, you haven't missed it! You'll know when it comes."

"How will I know?"

"You'll have lots of champagne! And a party."

And she did not miss it, as he promised. But there was so much to take in, so many faces she should recognise and mostly didn't, that Charles was disappointed to find that she didn't even recognise him. He'd been fond of her since the days in his childhood when she had boasted that she could handle him a good deal better than his mother. It was true, but she was probably unaware that he had her measure too. At all events they were good friends and Charles was sad to think that he had made such an effort to bring all his family to pay tribute and she didn't even realise it.

All good parties come to an end, and in due course the families dispersed. Charles hired a car and visited various friends and relatives, sweeping the country from south to north, so that Mum and Alex, going straight home, had time to complete their preparations. Alex hoovered while Mum dusted and between them they made up beds, turning on electric blankets to air them. There was still the problem of the central heating. The boiler was not working properly. Alex got worked up about it in vain.

"They'll have to manage without," he said, cursing his luck. "We've got lots of wood for the fire, electric fires and those two gas stoves. We'll have to make do."

Mum was appalled, but Alex mustn't get excited whatever happened.

"It'll be all right. Don't worry."

They persuaded themselves that all would be well, knowing that the top room was as cold as a barn at the best of times; this was mid-winter. As it happened they need not have worried. Charles took a look at the boiler as soon as he arrived, and being an engineer, coaxed it into action. It didn't help Alex's morale but it warmed the house. There was still something wrong with the boiler. It was noisy and it leaked smoke into the boiler room. As long as visitors were around Alex dare not turn the thing off in case it could not start again.

And there was another thing. Mum's standard of housework was not very creditable, in spite of her training in so prestigious a hospital. She had not, as her neighbours would have said, "bottomed" the place. Clean sheets and pillowcases, yes, but what about those pillows, which had not been in use for years? Full of house mites, without a doubt: she had forgotten Charles's asthma. Not only was the family chilled to the bone and suffering from asthma but the night seemed twice as long as they were used to.

And not a pin must drop or Alex's sleep pattern would be ruined, and who knew what disaster might follow? They suffered dutifully, all stepping round like cats on hot bricks, not daring to put a foot out of turn. Mum felt that it was up to her to cater for them all, feeling hamstrung in that it was not wholly her kitchen while Alex was around. Carol felt that she knew what her family wanted to eat and wished Mum would let her get on with it. At last they could stand it no longer and took themselves off to where there were young people.

There would be other much happier visits in time to come. But at least Alex had stayed the course and cleared another milestone. There was one very beneficial result of their stay.

"Alex," Charles asked one morning when they were all wondering what to do. "What happened to your trike?"

"I sold it to a chap in Barrowford."

"Do you think he's still got it?"

"I don't know."

"Shall we go and see?"

Alex had had a monumental clear out when he had come back from hospital to live at Higher Clough. He was convinced his life was over, that he would never need any of his tools, his collection of cars or even the trike again. Nothing that Mum could say would make him change his mind. He was going to sell up and clear out. He sold what he could and much of the rest he took in daily loads to the tip. It became, belatedly, a joke: anything that was missing had "gone to the tip". At the time Mum had a job to guard her possessions.

The menfolk, Charles, Alex and Robert went now in search of the trike. As luck would have it, it was still in the garage of the man who had bought it and he was glad enough to sell it back. It had been a special treasure in the days when, together with a friend from the Sanatorium, Alex had combined the front end of a motorbike with the back end of a Morris 1300. It was a good deal more powerful than an ordinary motorbike and went like the wind. Mum remembered seeing Alex's crash hat hurtling along the top of the hedge by Dandan's bungalow and wondering if he could stop in time. No trouble! The only thing, before he mastered it, was its tendency to do unsolicited "wheelies". But what fun he had on that machine.

It was a brilliant idea of Charles's. The one thing most obviously missing from Alex's life at present was fun. There was plenty of it while the brothers worked on restoring the neglected vehicle and more still when it was roadworthy with a 'Q' registration. It added a new dimension to Alex's life and remained a blessing long after the Australians returned home.

Chapter 19

Scotland

Mum received a letter from Dandan to her great astonishment. She had tried hard to make Dandan write to all the friends she had left behind when she came to live at John Peel's cottage. It was one of the few things she could still do. She had always maintained that she could not write – until she wanted Bim to find something for her in her old home. That had been a long clear letter with specific instructions. Too bad that Bim no longer had the key.

Mum was even more surprised when she opened the letter to read:

Dear Moll,

Thank you ever so much for the lovely party you gave me. It was very good of you...

You never knew with Dandan whether she were on the ball or not. By pretending to be confused she had, often enough, got away with blue murder. She never approached anything directly. She was feline in her inconsequential tangent-like approach to something upon which her mind was set like a vice. Was this letter a subtle reproach? Did she think Mum should have been giving the party? Should she be looking after her? Did she think, seeing Alex so well, that Mum would be free to look after her mother again? But Mum had tasted freedom. And who could think that Dandan would be better off anywhere else than where she was? She had the whole place revolving round her. They all loved her and thought her remarkable – which she undoubtedly was. Why come back to the little dog at the end of the leash, the only one aware of her clay feet?

Alex had been saving up to take Mum on a holiday in Scotland. As soon as the spring weather was warm enough they would go. They would follow their noses, stopping for bed and breakfast, wherever the fancy took them. Ultimately, they aimed for Lewes where they hoped to trace an ancestor Alexander MacKenzie. Mum was to leave her purse at home. Alex was paying all expenses. When the money ran out they would come home. Spring had come for everyone else too and they could hardly edge the car out of their lane into the traffic.

"This is no good at all!" Alex said in anguish, as every attempt was headed off. "If we ever get there, we shall be dead of exhaustion!"

"Why don't we turn left instead and get off the main road?"

They had a map and that is exactly what they did. They wove their way across country through the most beautiful, unexplored and unhurried scenery; finding themselves in Scotland, unruffled, as early as they would have done in the rat-race. They found their first B&B in Peebles with a pleasant efficient landlady who sent them off next day with a huge sustaining breakfast inside them. If this was breakfast they could do without lunch and make the holiday last longer. They were to find that breakfasts were as good all along the way.

They met some interesting people, which was an important part of the holiday, and saw some beautiful country, surely at its best? The young beech leaves were bursting out, with bluebells underneath; the gorse was more brilliant than any Mum had seen elsewhere and the birds were busy with their nests. Alex was adept at identifying them from their flight and songs. His greatest joy was spotting a pair of golden eagles. He caught sight of a kestrel. On the shoreline he was thrilled to see oystercatchers.

Skye was at its memorable best. The two weeks of fine weather that had recently been enjoyed, was breaking, so that they had the best of both worlds: sunshine followed by stormy rain, followed again by brilliant sunshine. The lights were unbelievable sometimes, especially in the evenings. They were artists' lights. Alex was torn with the desire to get busy with his brushes, yet knowing that the time was not yet. He took a great many photos, which were the next best thing.

Lewes, by contrast, they crossed to on a dull dour day and travelled the length of the island in gloom. There was little vegetation; little life of any sort, except for a thriving peat industry and a solitary plantation of conifers. However, by the time they reached Stornaway, the sun had come out to greet them and the place was as bright and lively as Skye.

After their wonderful holiday they began to wonder how Kathryn was getting on. Kathryn had been a patient when Alex was last in hospital. She had kindly written a letter for him to Mum. Mum was unable to visit since Alex had smashed her car in his attempt to get into hospital. They had been to see her once, neither she nor Alex being fully recovered. Her husband, a psychiatric nurse, was off work to look after her and the family. It was a modest home: no luxuries, no car, but there was an air of practical Christianity. It did not need the articles written by Kathryn, which she proudly showed Mum, but of which she was no longer capable, to convince Mum of that. Kathryn and Arthur spoke of their family who must have been a credit to any parents. There were four of them and at least one foster child.

They must have been wonderful parents. But it had been sad to see Kathryn so lacking in energy and confidence. That was a year or so ago. Mum telephoned.

"Kathryn, how are you?"

"I'm alright thanks. How are you?"

"Alex and I wondered whether we could come and see you again?"

"Yes."

"Can we come this afternoon?" No need to ask if she would be in; poor Kathryn had little option.

They found her and Arthur a little under the weather but ready with a welcoming cup of tea. They told them of their holiday, Mum feeling horribly uncomfortable. How could they talk of holidays when these two so obviously needed one? What possible chance did they stand of getting one? Kathryn confessed to feeling depressed. She had been thinking of going back to hospital. What a place to think of spending a holiday!

"How would you like to come and stay with us?"

Kathryn was embarrassed. She would never have thought of such a thing. Leaving the security of home and Arthur's care was one thing; going to a strange house to strange people was another. She could not think of it.

"Oh, I couldn't," she said at once. "I couldn't leave my family!"

"But you'd be leaving them if you went to hospital. Couldn't you try it?"

"It's very kind of you, but I couldn't, really."

Mum turned to Arthur: "Have you got a car?"

"No, but I can borrow one."

"Well, why don't you and Kathryn come over to lunch one day? Bring her night case and, if you both like the look of the place and think she would be happy with us, you could leave her. She wouldn't have to stay a minute longer than she wanted to. We could always bring her back or you could come and fetch her. And she could always ring you up at any time. We can't say fairer than that, now can we?"

She turned to beam at Kathryn, who was beginning to weaken.

Two days later they came and approved. Kathryn stayed voluntarily for a week and the change did her a power of good. She had found little energy to help Arthur with the chores at home but was now on best behaviour: she helped Mum wash up, peel the potatoes and so on. They even did together some of the jobs that Mum might not have considered necessary, were she not also on her best behaviour! With Alex they went for little drives to favourite haunts, and for walks and pottered about in the garden.

One day, when out in the car, they passed a house that was for sale.

"Stop!" said Kathryn, surprisingly. "I was brought up in that house!"

Since it was for sale there was nothing to stop them going up the drive. She told them how it used to be when she was a child. There had been a large beautifully kept garden in those days where they had played hide-and-seek. The garden was sadly neglected now; she felt no regrets for days gone by.

Alex asked Kathryn before she went, if she still kept going back to the hospital for injections, as he had been asked to do? Yes, she supposed the doctors must know best.

"Why don't you try going without, Kathryn? I wouldn't take them and look at me now!

"I don't want to undermine your faith, Kathryn, but I do wonder at times if the doctors have the answer. I don't see how they can myself because they don't take into account the spirit of man. Mental health professionals don't appear to recognise the spirit or even acknowledge it. This is more a spiritual disease than a mental one in my view. Why don't you try it?"

"I think perhaps I will."

"You talk it over with Arthur. As long as you have his support you'll be all right."

It was a month or two before they met her again and by that time she was writing articles and back in charge of her kitchen.

Chapter 20

Craftsman

Not long after this incident Mum heard from her agent, who had undertaken to try and redeem the mess left by the builders when they came to her remaining cottage. Another builder was hard to find and enthusiasm was at a low ebb. But there was a housing boom and the estate agent proposed placing the cottage on the market. It was surprising and disappointing that his asking price was considerably less than she had been led to expect two years before the housing boom. She was in no mood to argue. Get it gone at any price. Cut her losses. She accepted the first modest offer.

A month later – she was accustomed to legal sloth –she rang the lawyer to ask how things were going.

"Offer? What offer? I do remember, let me see…yes, here it is. I never heard any more about it." Back to square one. It was exasperating sitting here doing nothing, leaving other people to get on with your business and finding that they were doing nothing too. Mum felt that she *must* go up and sort the matter out herself. Alex was so much better now. Perhaps I (also much better these days) would come and look after him and Mum could stay with Les for a few days to sort out her cottage problems.

"We eat our main meal of fish and vegetables at noon on the dot and have a great variety of salad at five o'clock. I can't see this fitting in with your working day at Ruthwaite, Mum. We work on the processor in the mornings and go for a walk in the afternoons."

No, Mum was not interested in diets or nutrition or exercise, but her problem remained. Alex took pity on his mother. She was like a peregrine falcon that would plummet at 35 miles an hour to catch a starling and tear it in four for her four newly hatched chicks. Each time Mum sold property she would divide the profits into four for us chicks. She'd given away most of the money her property had realised; this last cottage was to be her own nest egg. It was a bit hard if no one could help her now. All right! He would help her.

"Why don't we both go up and have a look?"

"Oh, Alex!" She wouldn't have asked him, but since he had suggested it… "That would be excellent! Do you really feel up to it?"

"Well, we can have a go, can't we? I don't like to see my old Mum left in the lurch."

After lunching with us they went to see the cottage. It looked very different from when Mum had last seen it. The bathroom over the kitchen had been completed, but at the expense of the lean-to shed, which no longer existed. That shed would have been important to Mum: essential as somewhere to keep coal, wood and garden tools. She was upset. They'd used this stone when there was plenty of demolition stone available. There being no ground of her own, the original demolition stone had been left on neighbouring waste ground and later bulldozed in by the neighbour with whom she failed to conclude the contract.

It was not just the missing shed. Where the ground had fallen away beyond it, leaving room only for access by barrow to the rear, was now a much-used private thoroughfare where she had hoped to park her cars. There was just room for a steep bank and narrow path to her own tiny back garden.

The front door, formed to take a stone porch, was lined with concrete blocks rising to an arch at the top. The new bank forming the driveway cut the corner of the building so fine that if the porch were built there would be no access to the rear. If it were not built the place would look absurd. They would have to remove the concrete blocks and settle for a slate canopy.

They went in through the brand new front door.

"Funny," said Mum, "what happened to the one Donald put in?" (They found it later in use somewhere else.)

There were no doors separating the hall from the sitting room, the kitchen or the cloakroom. In the sitting room there were, apparently, the remains of a junkyard. Several bedsteads had never made it to the sale, nor had any other woebegone pieces and part pieces of furniture. Part bags of solid cement, bits of plaster and plaster dust, cigarette packets, broken tea-stained mugs and coke bottles were strewn all over the floor.

There was the fire grate that Mum had bought, but still no fireplace. In the kitchen, stranded in the middle of the room, was the sink unit, which should have been connected to the new Rayburn, which had been installed while Mum was still there. The rest of the kitchen units, one of her last purchases, were installed and gave satisfaction. But lying among the assorted rubbish on the floor was the ragged, torn, filthy vinyl that had once been her pride and joy. It had been kept outside and was fit now only for the dustbin. There was also an electric cooker, which she realised had once gleamed in John Peel's cottage: another candidate for the skip.

Upstairs was not too bad; that had been pretty well finished before she left. The bath was back to front in her opinion. She had designed it so as to look out of the window at one of the best views, while soaking in the tub. The plan had also been practical in that there was a minimum of pipes needed, an economy in itself, and an efficient hot water system. She had bought all that was necessary but an awful lot more had been bought since in her name. The radiators were all in place but not all were connected. It should be a matter of minutes to finish the job and then they could turn the water on and start work.

Right away they found a broom and cleared the worst of the mess. There was a double bed and mattress, which seemed to be in fairly good order when they'd beaten the dust out of it. It didn't seem to be damp. If they got the electricity turned on they could bring electric blankets and bedclothes. There were two or three single beds, so Mum had her pick; Alex needed the double one to cater for his length.

First, they had to go and see the agent and arrange for the electricity to be connected. She had paid for this over a year previously but the men had put their meter in a locked box on the outside of the house, which nobody could open. Nor did there seem to be a working unit inside. Something had to be sorted there.

Mum was surprised to see a new face at the estate agent's. Her old friend, who had taken pity on her plight and tried to get the job finished, had gone. No wonder the whole thing had lapsed. One could hardly expect a new agent to look kindly on such a project. Perhaps he was relieved to hear that she and Alex now proposed to improve matters. He assured them that the market was still good and that, anyway, there would always be a demand for a converted barn, so there was no great hurry. Fine! They would come up in a few days' time, spend a couple of nights and see what could be done.

On the following Sunday they packed tools, food, clothes, bedclothes, hot water bottles and an electric Baby Belling, kettle and pans, a couple of folding chairs and a portable TV. They could have stayed for a week but Alex was not up to that yet. I filled their bottles and gave them a good meal. They arrived at the cottage ready for anything.

Still no electricity, and of course, no water. But the water did not matter since the stopcock was just outside and Mum had put an outside tap for the next cottage. The new owner allowed them to draw from it. With this and some plaster he had brought with him, Alex was able to make good all the missing plaster: nothing seemed to be quite finished anywhere. He was in charge and getting his old form back.

In the afternoon they drove to the old quarry and found some suitable stone for the fireplace; bought sand and cement and he set about building an attractive surround and hearth. Mum meanwhile was going about in a dream, using cold water, Jif and a knife to clean the cooker and fridge. No one would want to buy them but if they were in place they could give the buyer an idea of size. And if they were not too foul, they might be an asset rather than a deterrent.

After a long day of hard work they supped with us. We always found Alex's accounts of progress entertaining. He and Les sparred well together. They stayed till late. Reaching the front door, Alex felt in his pocket for the key. He couldn't find it.

"What have you done with the key?"

"I haven't done anything with it! You know I never lock anything up!"

"I seem to have lost it. What on earth have I done with it?"

It dawned on him that he had worn his new jacket when visiting Les and me. There were so few social occasions to sport such things that it had seemed to be a good idea. He'd never thought to take the key out.

They didn't feel they could come back to Caldbeck. We had no spare rooms anyway. They'd have to find a B&B. Mum racked her brains. She recalled that the nearby rectory had converted into a guesthouse. They later discovered that it was a hotel and took two single rooms en suite, both comfortable. They had a much better breakfast than they would otherwise have done and were in time to meet the potential array of workmen.

They need not have hurried. The electrician came first, an old friend who explained that he still had the consumer unit to put in and a cable connecting it to the box outside. He had thought that with the house being empty it was safer to leave it disconnected. Fair enough. It was good to see him again. The plumber came next, in his suit.

"Are you going to connect us up straight away, so that we can get some work done?"

"I can't do that! I'll have to have a look first and see what wants doing."

"I can tell what needs doing," said Mum desperately. "Look, it's only this sink unit and one or two radiators not connected properly."

"Let's have a look, shall we?" He proceeded to examine the position thoroughly. It took a long time.

"I expect you'd like me to send you an estimate?"

"Have you any idea how much it's going to cost?" she said feebly.

"No, I can't tell you until I've worked it all out."

"And you can't possibly get our water supply going while we are here?"

"I'll send you an estimate as soon as I can, but I can't start work till next week."

So that was that.

"I'd better give you our address then."

It was bitterly disappointing. And still no Electricity Board. Alex and Mum took themselves off to find tiles for kitchen, bathroom and cloakroom. They found some real beauties, which cheered them up. When they returned, there was the Electricity Board's van across the road.

"Have you come to connect us?" she asked through the window, enthusiasm restored once more.

"Nothing to do with us, love. Hasn't he been? I thought he said he was coming out here this morning."

"Perhaps he has been, while we were out," crestfallen.

They went into the cottage. Mum put on the hall light. Nothing. Alex went through to the kitchen and turned on the light. Nothing.

"He hasn't been! He can't have been and gone away as if we weren't here, can he?"

At that moment the fluorescent light blazed in the kitchen after a moment of delayed reaction. Things were looking up. The hall light bulb needed changing. After a sandwich lunch and coffee – *hot* coffee, they got down to a bit more work. Alex did the skilled job: tiling, while Mum tried to make something of the path and bank outside.

They were quite cosy that evening with a hot meal, a fire to sit by and the TV to watch. The cloakroom tiles looked beautiful, but Alex coveted the kitchen tiles for Higher Clough. The bathroom needed new plaster before the tiles could be fixed. The next job was to get timber for the porch roof. Alex succeeded in putting this together before they knocked off for another rest.

On their next return they brought three magnificent matching doors for the hall. Alex put up the architraves and hung them. Mum painted them. They went to town to buy brass furniture for them. Once again Alex was struck with how nice they would look on his doors back home. They bought enough for both. After all, the labourer was worthy of his hire and Alex was doing this out of the goodness of his heart. While they were in town they looked for carpets and kitchen floor covering and arranged for a man to come and measure. May as well be hanged for a sheep as a lamb. That sitting room would certainly look better covered, and the kitchen was a must.

They would come up again in a fortnight's time, as before, for a couple of nights. Mum thought it expedient to see her bank manager now that she was spending money so rapidly: he must be hoping for his share. He was unable to come before they returned again, but agreed to come to lunch. She made the appointment over the phone, so wrote the directions to make it easier for him to find. And away they went. They got on splendidly with gathering strength. A load of gravel was delivered to spread over the front and along the path to the back. They had the fence to make; carpets to lay; slates for the porch and the rest of the tiling to do. Alex was excelling at every task. Surely, they could do all this in one go and finish for good?

"Yes, let's do that," said Alex. "I feel fine!"

So they finished the job, called in the agent to have a look and were delighted to find that it would be worthwhile to auction it. There were several interested buyers with whom he was happy to keep in touch. The only snag was that there was a postal strike. Usually, one advertised an auction for three weeks, but it would not be fair to go ahead in view of the strike.

This was disappointing but he knew that they had been racing slowly against time and that the cottage was supposed to have been saleable six months earlier: the sellers' market must be almost at an end. They left him to make the arrangements and went home to open their mail. There was one from the bank manager thanking Mum for her directions and looking forward to seeing her on the 21st.

"It'll be nice to see him again," Mum said. "Wait a moment, 21st? What's the date today? Did you say the 28th? Wow! How am I going to laugh my way out of that one? He'll probably call in my overdraft!"

"I'd forgotten all about him."

"So had I. How absolutely dreadful. We got carried away I never thought we could stick so long a stint. But I'm glad we did. I'll have to make my peace somehow."

She had visions of the poor man going without his lunch.

"He'd be alright. He could always pop into The Moorcock Inn."

She rang the bank in the morning, abject.

"Kenneth? How can I apologise? You did come to lunch last Thursday?"

"Yes, I came. I could see you were away by all your mail."

It hadn't been worth stopping for a couple of nights.

"We didn't expect to be away so long; we'd only managed two days at a time until now. This time we thought we could keep going, so we did. I am so sorry."

"That's alright. I knew something must have happened. How's it going then?"

"It's really finished at last! It will be auctioned in about three weeks' time, so I should be solvent by then. You won't know me!"

"Perhaps I can advise you what to do with your unaccustomed wealth?"

"Thanks. I'd better get it first. But you must admit it looks more promising. An auction does mean instant cash doesn't it? It looks as if we might be lucky and do really well, if the market will just hang out that long."

"I'll look forward to seeing you then."

That was a relief. He had always been very good to her, but anyone can be tried too high.

A fortnight passed, the postal strike soon over and no word from the agent. Mum phoned.

"Oh! Did you want to sell? I've been waiting to hear from you."

Mum was speechless. There seemed to be a serious flaw in her communication system.

"Of course I want to sell. You know how we have been racing against the market. You came over a fortnight ago and arranged to auction it as soon as the postal strike was over. It was over almost at once. What happened?"

"I suppose I had better arrange for an auction now, then? Let me see, that should be three weeks from next Saturday. Would that be all right?"

Nearly another month. Ye gods!

"I suppose it will have to be. Do you think there is any chance of the market holding on that long?"

"I don't see why not. We had a very good sale last Saturday."

So be it.

The anxious vigil ended in a beautiful autumn day, the sort when nothing can possibly go wrong. Alex and Mum revelled in the sunshine and autumn colours as they drove in eager anticipation of this climax to so many endeavours. With any luck they might do really well. They had nothing to be ashamed of in their work. Alex had enjoyed perfecting his skills in stonework, carpentry, tiling and plastering. They felt smugly that they deserved to make a fortune.

It was due to start at 2.00pm. They arrived in plenty of time, meeting Les and me for lunch in the bar in view of the entrance to the hotel. They heard a woman at the reception desk asking where the auction was to be held.

"She's a keen buyer," Mum whispered, not hearing the answer but there was plenty of time. They need only wait for the agent, who must come through that door. Time slipped by. There was very little activity at the door. Mum went up to the reception desk.

"Can you tell me where the auction is to be held this afternoon?"

"Auction, madam? There is no auction here today."

"But my house is to be auctioned today! Have we come to the wrong hotel? Do they hold auctions anywhere else?"

"We usually hold them here, madam, but we have none today. We had a very good one last week. There were a lot of people here. I believe they had a very good sale."

"I can't understand it."

At that moment the agent came in with the auctioneer. They went over to the desk. Mum moved towards them.

"What has happened?" she asked.

"Good afternoon, Mrs Dalglish," the auctioneer was unperturbed. "There seems to be a slight misunderstanding," he smiled. "They have put us in a different room. Would you come this way?"

The six of us walked through into a small room at the back. The woman whom Mum had heard inquiring was eating her sandwiches. They talked perfunctorily until the auctioneer said they'd better begin. A man came in. Could he be a buyer?

"Ladies and gentlemen, please bear with me while I read through the regulations.... Do I have an offer?"

What offer?

"Was that an offer, madam?"

The woman looked terrified and bolted. Never in all the years she had attended auctions, by way of free entertainment, had she been so embarrassed. The man, who was killing time before a meeting, ambled away.

The auctioneer turned to Mum: "I'm afraid we do not have a sale."

There was no point stopping to argue why not. Obviously this firm was not going to sell her cottage for

177

her. The boom was over. They were only here for the day. She must go to another agent. Perhaps it didn't do to mention one's deserts to *fate*: she had a nasty habit of thinking differently – and always had the last laugh.

The next agent was encouraging.

"Yes, we're still doing quite a lot of business. I must say I am amazed to hear that you can't sell such a property as yours. It sounds highly desirable."

This agent very soon reported three buyers, vying with each other, and Mum accepted a better offer than she could have hoped for. As always, there's many a slip…for one reason or another it was six months before a contract was signed and the figure had shrunk considerably.

Even if she had lost money over it, it would have been worth all the effort. Not only was it satisfactory to Mum to finish the job well that she had started so long ago, but the boost it had given to Alex's morale was worth everything. He had faced up to the old scene of horror. The locals no longer looked askance at him, but with respect for his ability as a craftsman, and as a man who looks after his mother.

Alex could now lift up his head. He could do a full day's work. His sleep pattern was unsettled but there was no cause for anxiety. He would not go off the rails. Above all, he did not have to resort to taking Largactil, though he would have taken it if need be. He felt pleased with himself, and so he should. Mum was immensely proud of him.

Chapter 21

Death Game

After their mammoth operations on the cottage, Alex and Mum eased off, gathering strength to tackle all the outstanding jobs at Higher Clough. Alex completed two-way steps to the garden. He built a stone arch over the passage; he improved the boundary walls and made a style on the top boundary so that he and Stan could visit each other with ease.

He had in mind to build an octagonal summerhouse on the viewpoint, a patio round the pond and a greenhouse: monumental tasks if contemplated as a whole, but he approached small sections at a time, perfecting each piece of the jigsaw before tiring of it. He obtained the satisfaction of achievement for each segment. Then, exhausted by that project he would start on another and renew his joy. It worried Mum at first thinking that he was never going to finish anything. But she learned in time that he always finished in the end and never risked getting bored or defeated, always keeping his standards supremely high. Nagging would not have helped.

It was slow progress. But what did it matter? He was not yet able to compete in the commercial world. But his contribution of effort was second to none. And, in his own way, he was gradually rehabilitating himself.

They found a lad with a rotary cultivator who would come and lay out the kitchen garden.

"It's no good doing that!" Stan said. "You'll cut up all the weeds and have ten times as many! It will have to be forked over first."

Mum was discouraged. She had bargained with the lad for a price and had been pleasantly surprised. However, he knew his job and brought a fork with him, unasked. He made a splendid job of it, turning in what topsoil they could muster and a lot of "good stuff" from the farmer. They had seen a programme on TV promoting the idea of four-foot wide beds bordered with timber, with two-foot wide paths between. This way you kept your feet clean and didn't compact the soil. The paths were covered with black polythene and gravel. No weeds. They had a magnificent crop of vegetables the first year, but the "breathtaking" array of azaleas and heathers in front of the house perished. Who could blame them? They had no nourishment, but were re-established the following year.

Alex brought out his trike into the open again. It was not reliable enough to be worth spending money on but it was fun. He often sped off to buy a paper in Barnoldswick. One day he ran out of petrol and a man stopped to give him a lift. He'd noticed him on this strange vehicle before and invited him in for a cup of tea. He and his wife were pensioners, neither of them too well but very hospitable. Alex was delighted. He needed new friends.

Greg was waiting to go into hospital for exploratory tests. Alex called on several occasions, liking them both very much. One day he called to find that Greg had returned from hospital with not very cheering news of himself, but worse, his wife must have known in her heart what the verdict would be: she had not waited for confirmation but had died before he came back. Their daughter came to look after him and Alex did his best to lend support and sympathy.

In this very same week news came that Dandan was ill. Mum had planned in any case to visit her the week after. It was soon after Christmas 1989. For the first time in her life, Dandan had not been in the bosom of her family for the event. Bim and Stella had gone to live on the Isle of Wight and could not manage it. Mum had written to commiserate, assuring Dandan that she must have had a wonderful time in the home. But she felt uncomfortable about it. Would Dandan have taken this as a suggestion that she was losing her grip? She had been half expecting to hear something of this sort.

She rang the home.

"I understand Mrs Longridge is not so well today?"

"She is not at all well, I'm afraid."

"I had planned to come next week to see her. Do you think I should come sooner?"

"Well, it is up to you of course, but in my opinion she is dying."

Strong words. There could be no option then.

Mum was Dandan's executor and had expected her mother to live forever. After all, there was no reason why she should ever wear out, or rust out. She was caught on the wrong foot. There must be documents she should have at her fingertips. But what? She rummaged through her drawers and came across the old diary she had written in time of her despair and frustration while living with Dandan in her bungalow. She opened the page and saw the words: "She's done it again! And she catches me out every time!"

This referred to a time when Alex had been invited to stay with a friend in America and Dandan had not wanted him to go. She had never said anything of course; she never did. But about ten days before he was due to go they found her in bed one morning on the point of death. Mum sent for the doctor who prescribed sips of brandy whenever she wanted it. Brandy! Presently, Dandan made her understand that she would prefer Dubonnet. Perhaps Mum had maligned her, but she appeared to be reacting in her dramatic way to Alex's holiday.

If she were right, Dandan had made the fatal mistake of starting too soon. This was quite in character. Had she not always arrived to dinner parties ten minutes early, when Mum had only allowed seven minutes to make the gravy and change her clothes, thus throwing the whole party into disarray? Grimly Mum removed Dandan's sleeping pills from their usual place the night before Alex's departure. She could hardly sleep that night and inevitably heard the

181

usual footsteps along to the cloakroom. At fever pitch she listened for the returning footsteps. They proceeded to the kitchen. There was the sound of drawers and cupboards opening and shutting. She was right.

"I've got 'em here, my dear," she muttered triumphantly.

Dandan was in her usual excellent health in the morning.

Remembering this and all the other times when she had been caught out, Mum wondered now whether it was another grand stage production. Dandan always liked to have something interesting going on. Or had she decided that it was time to call it a day? It would not be the same without her.

She and Alex travelled down soberly. Alex was understandably in a highly emotional state, having so recently lost his new friend and being about to lose another, to say nothing of Dandan, who had always been special to him since his happy days with her at the bungalow. These last years of estrangement had wounded him as well as her.

They reached the home to find Bim and Stella and others of his family seated or standing round the bed. Dandan was lying with her head back and mouth open. She looked dreadful! How would Al take it? She had forgotten that he would have been concerned with such sights as a night porter. Not much good trying to get round the bed to kiss her. They loitered uncomfortably until the matron came in with a nurse to make the bed comfortable. They talked quietly about Dandan, Mum expressing the opinion that she was not finished yet and recalled her finding of the diary. Dandan's arms flailed the bedclothes, but what of that? She was unconscious. They all knew that.

It was not till later that the significance of that gesture dawned on Mum. It was over thirty years since Dandan had had one of those *turns* when she knew what was going on but appeared to be unconscious and could do nothing.

Last time it had happened Mum had called her bluff and it had never happened since. Thirty years! But what about today? Was this not exactly the same thing again? Mum was appalled. What had she said, thinking her mother unconscious? She had revealed a truth that nobody wanted to hear, and with which Dandan would now, knowingly, have to live.

Bim had been staying overnight at the home and would again since Mum had travelled so far, but Mum insisted that it was her turn. They prepared a bed for her but she preferred to stay by her mother's side. Some of the nurses came in to take their leave of a favourite patient before the weekend. They hardly expected to see her again. Sister came in and paid tribute to her indomitable spirit. She and Mum agreed that whether Dandan lived or died, it would be of her own choosing.

"She's never lost a battle in her life," Mum said, "except, perhaps, to be given a bath! And I don't believe she lost that one till she came here!"

"Ah well," said Sister reminiscently smiling, "that's one you can't win, isn't it?"

For the next twenty-four hours Dandan struggled for life, attended by anxious family and devoted staff. Though still unconscious she had managed to convey to each watcher, by a squeeze of her hand, that all was well with them. Mum held her hand through much of the night but there was no such reassurance for her. Had Dandan heard? Did she know her cover was blown? The second night Mum felt sure that Dandan did know that she was all right, but she was not going to forgive her. Mum left the bedside and slept on the bed provided. In the morning the night nurses got Dandan out of bed while they made it. Evidently, she had decided to live.

Mum, still smarting from not being forgiven said brusquely, "Well, there's no point all of us hanging around here. Alex and I are going home."

The family was outraged! What appallingly bad taste! How could Mum be so heartless? She wondered herself.

"What else can we do but go home?" she asked Theresa, who was putting them up. "We shall be wrong whatever we do! She's got us on a string and can give it a yank whichever way we go."

Theresa understood Mum's frustration but was shocked nonetheless.

"It sounds as if you were discussing a pitched battle, rather than a death scene," she remarked mildly.

Mum was glad to get Alex away from all this drama. They travelled home uneventfully until they reached their own cattle grid. On it was sitting a neighbour in his Land Rover.

"Have you been away?" he asked.

"Yes, we've been down to see my grandmother."

"I thought you must have been. You've been broken into. I'm just waiting here to direct the police."

"Thanks very much. What's happened?"

"The Jehovah's Witnesses have just been to our place. They'd been to you first and found the door bust in. You'd better go and see. I'll wait here."

Sure enough, the door had been kicked in. Dazed, they looked around inside to see what was missing. Obviously, the portable TV in the kitchen. That was the newest article they had and the most saleable. Nothing else, apparently, had been considered worth taking. There was a cupboard in which everything had been moved but not scattered. Probably someone had been looking for money. They'd have been lucky to find any! Alex missed the gold stopwatch given to him by his father for his twenty-first birthday. He was sure it had been in that cupboard, but found it later elsewhere.

It was a rotten homecoming. After the trauma in Sussex, and Alex's other worries, they could have done without the series of police calls and searches. One man had a look round outside but it was dark by then and he saw nothing untoward.

Alex on the other hand had got his dander up. He very much resented being broken into. He scratched his name on the remaining TV set and anything remotely likely to have been overlooked and still vulnerable. He had a look around outside and found a notable tyre print in the mud outside the top cattle grid, suggesting that someone had come up the drive and, instead of turning outside the house where they might have found it necessary to escape through the bottleneck of the cattle grid, they had reversed in the drive, ready for a hasty exit.

Poor old Sherlock Holmes! Alex followed this trail all day, leading him as it did at first, red-faced to his own trike! But it could not have been that. The trike had not been there for a start, though it was a similar make of tyre. This was a newer one, making a very firm clear print. He followed it down to the drive and on down the lane. What was that, across the road parked in his neighbour's driveway? A brand new tyre of the right make! But it was on the wrong side! No, it wasn't though! If the car had been in reverse, it would have been on that side. He must tell the police. While he waited for them to come a neighbour walked past. Alex explained his presence.

"That? Oh, that belongs to Mrs Alsop who used to live here. She was round here yesterday. She ran out of petrol and left her car there."

End of excitement.

Alex went to see his friend and daughter. The old man was showing fortitude but it was a sad household. Mum had rung the residential home first thing and been told that her mother was still very ill.

"I'm sure she will recover," Mum said. "She had turned the corner when we left and she was never one to look back!"

"I hope you're right."

Dandan's life hung in the balance. She must have decided that if her manoeuvres were recognised, the game was no longer worth playing. Bim rang to tell his sister that it was all over. Mum felt stricken. The lifelong battle between herself and her mother was ended. What a sad and sordid end. Mum had been convinced that Dandan would

185

recover to fight again. She would have won again, as she always did, and made Mum cross once more. She had given up at last, when she had already won! In this had she not triumphed finally in making Mum wrong with an inexorable finality?

Bim asked Mum what she would like for the funeral hymn. Mum flippantly suggested "fight the good fight", and was surprised to be taken literally. But everyone who knew Dandan felt this to be a suitable choice. The family foregathered for the funeral from far and wide. There was a cousin living near Robert Schuster with whom Alex and Mum both stayed. Ed wanted to go to Dandan's funeral but would have found it difficult to go on his own. He was glad to go with Robert, Mum and Alex. Alex was particularly glad to have his company since Ed, having his own troubles, needed support more than Alex did.

Mum nearly decided not to go to the funeral. She had thought it much too taxing for Alex and she did not feel that she could leave him at this time. She said she was not going but the family was so shocked that Alex felt that he must steel himself and accompany his mother. And so they went, taking Ed under their wing.

Alex was in a state of "gallant, high-hearted happiness" as they set off on their mission. He looked after Ed, helped him smarten his appearance, saw to it that he was not left on his own and warned Mum when he felt that Ed had had all he could take. She collected her little party to make a discreet exit. When they reached Ed's home, Alex refused to go any further until he was sure Ed could get in. It was just as well he did wait. Ed was locked out, his lodger having taken the key.

Ed knew where the lodger was likely to be and phoned him. His lodger suggested that he should break a window: Alex took over the phone and told him that they would be coming to get the key. It was handed over reluctantly and Ed seen safely inside his own house. Next morning Alex insisted on seeing if he were all right before they continued their journey home. Mum purred to see Alex so responsible and concerned for others.

On this high note, life continued for some weeks. Alex kept an eye on Greg and his daughter, giving a hand when he could. Otherwise it was all hands to the garden. They stayed once more with Robert and Alex went over on his own to see Ed. He came back with bad news. The house was empty: it had been broken into. A neighbour told him that Ed was back in mental hospital. Alex had spent the morning cleaning up and wondered if Mum would like to give him a hand with this onerous task.

They washed and scrubbed surfaces and crockery. Alex repaired the door. How could they help him? They decided to bring him home with them to make a fresh start. The hospital staff said it was fine for him to go but he must be back to appear in court next week. The reason for this was not very clear; there were several possibilities. In fact, Ed had got himself into considerable trouble and was delighted to have a change.

They hoped to persuade him to leave his house empty, the better to sell later if he decided to stay elsewhere. One of his lodgers (who had told Ed to break into his own house), was in hospital with him and unlikely to be released at present; another Ed had dismissed, and the third was away, his whereabouts unknown. They left a message for him to contact the hospital.

Higher Clough was a surprise to Ed. He justified his own garden by saying that he preferred it wild. Whereas Alex's orderly beds and paths spoke with promise of things to come, Ed's spoke without enthusiasm of what had been and no longer was. For a moment on arrival Ed's heart leapt with hope. It would be amazing to live like this! To leave all those sickening squabbles behind, those so-called friends who took advantage of him, and the police. Alex and Ed's aunt would know how to deal with them. They knew how to treat people decently. The first week was bliss.

Ed, who had not done anything constructive for a very long time, did what he could to help them as they pottered along with their chores. After each small effort he need a cigarette. Alex hated the smell of smoke but let him use the dining room to smoke in. They ate in the kitchen. In view of the court appearance, Mum persuaded the dentist to find time to refurbish his depleted set of dentures. Alex took him to his own tailor: Oxfam, where they found an excellent suit in which to present the new and improved image. Ed was delighted. He would knock them all cold! It was with some excitement that they appeared together. Everyone was as helpful as could be. There had to be further appearances when the lawyers had done their work, but the bench was anxious to inconvenience all concerned as little as possible. They couldn't believe their luck! They and Ed had been making problems for each other for too long. They now thought that they could see a happy ending for one of their regulars.

All this time Alex was still on his high, feeling responsible for the world around him and able to carry the weight. Mum remembered the power that drove him when he was evacuating Dandan from John Peel's cottage. It was frightening then but now it was under control and wholly good. Such power is transient and cannot be sustained indefinitely, nor can it be summoned at will. The thing is to make use of it when it is available. Alex was beginning to tire.

Stan came round one afternoon, as he often did, with more plants for the garden. He was beginning to fill their wide-open space.

"Stan, how nice to see you! What have you brought us this time? You are so generous. Did you notice the ajuga? It's spreading already!"

Mum put the kettle on. She knew just how he liked his tea.

"Oh! You've brought another hydrangea! We shall soon have the bank covered with them. I hope you've kept some for yourself?"

Ed walked through the kitchen on his way upstairs.

"Want a cup of tea, Ed?"

"Not now, thanks."

"You're not really going to keep him on here, are you?" Stan tried not to show how concerned he was.

"I don't know. The gilt is wearing off the gingerbread, but…"

"It wouldn't be fair to Alex! You must put him first, surely?"

"Of course I must, but you know it was Alex who suggested it. We both felt that we were so lucky, it was up to us to help anybody we could. We just followed our instincts. It would be so wonderful to help him find his real self."

"But it is destroying Alex. You can't do that."

"I know. I should have remembered that as far as moods are concerned: what goes up must come down! But who else could help him?"

"He's beyond help, surely?"

"I can't believe that anyone is beyond help! It is the old down-and-out syndrome. Nobody recognises the beauty behind the beast. I can't help feeling that all those poor souls in mental hospitals are potential geniuses that have never understood themselves or found anyone to understand them. Look at all the artists and musicians we know it has happened to. It is such a tragic waste of the most gifted people there are. All they need is love and patience and understanding."

"Do you think Ed is any better here?"

"I think he saw a brief vision of hope, but the idea of sustained effort appalls him. The incentive is not great enough. It's hard to remember that Alex went through a similar stage, and easy to lose patience. He's always had life too easy. Alex has his own fierce discipline. Ed's parents, both disciplined people at the top of their profession, when faced with an offspring who didn't quite fit, fell into the trap of overindulgence. It's easily done.

The only way to help people is to help them help themselves."

In the event it was Ed who found the way out. There were no rewards here. He didn't enjoy smoking alone; Alex didn't enjoy pub-crawling. There was no chance of cannabis or riotous living; in fact, nothing to look forward to. He rang his home number and found the third lodger at home. He had returned from abroad and let himself in with his own key. Ed greeted him with relief.

"Don't go away again," he said. "I'm coming back."

Mum heard him and was herself relieved.

Chapter 22

Wigton

Lithium carbonate kept me stable. I hadn't been in hospital for several years, benefitting from my regular meetings with Dr Srinivassan. Although Les only slept two hours a night after a naked run round the garden at midnight, I was always in bed by ten o'clock and slept at least eight hours. He spent many of his wakeful hours reading. When I wasn't cleaning and repairing oriental rugs, we worked together on the word processor in the mornings and often walked together or gardened in the afternoons. Many of the friends he had in his group called to consult him, sometimes about their marriages, sometimes about climbing mountains. He often threw the coins for a reading from the I Ching, the Chinese book of changes. I remember Aunt D valuing her copy in her library in the Borrowdale cottage.

I worked hard on the maintenance of both households and enjoyed preparing for the holidaymakers who came to my idyllic flat by the stream. But I began to feel that it was not going to be big enough for me to retire to. The bungalow would be far too expensive for me in this exclusive region. However, Wigton, six miles away was not in the National Park and had a certain stigma due to the presence of a silicon factory. Driving to town one day we noticed a house for sale, a 1930's detached house with a south-facing flat containing a mature Black Hamburg vine. The farmer's grandfather had built the house on the corner of the farm with views in four directions, two now obscured by housing estates. On the south side there was an open stretch of countryside towards the fells. The north and south conservatories were full of geraniums and fuchsias. The greenhouse behind the flat housed a younger vine with more tannin in the grape skins.

The place was near enough to the town centre to walk to the shops. What struck us particularly was its nearness to the library. Les was thinking once more of the books he must write. For this he needed access to a library. At present he was limited by the weekly library van. This was the bait for Les who otherwise would have been happy to stay in his charming bungalow close to his family and friends.

For me this house and garden were paradise! I would give everything I had to secure it! Maybe it was worth twice the sum of the flat, but I was undeterred. We took ourselves off to see Mum and Alex, determined not to mention the matter, at any rate until after lunch, but I was so bubbling over with excitement that before the meal was on the table it had all come out: this ideal house, which was so exactly what we needed. Mum raised her eyebrows. She turned to Les.

"What do you think of it, Les?"

Les made a helpless gesture.

"If Sally wants it, I wouldn't stand in her way. It would certainly be very handy to walk down to the library."

"How on earth could you afford it?" Mum asked me brutally.

"Well. Er..."

"Oh no!" Mum got the message. "I've got an overdraft already! Nothing doing, I'm sorry."

Mum rather feared that that would be the end of my dreams and hated to bring me back down to earth, but my determination was not thwarted.

"All right, if you can't help me, I'll do it myself. We must have that house. Les needs it to be near the library."

Little more was said that day. They didn't like to see me bashing my head against a brick wall. What chance could I have of buying such a place? They volunteered to come up and view the house. The short drive onto a double bend was off-putting. Alex vetted the place carefully. His intuition made him shrink. He noticed that the roof of the little north conservatory was made of fire escape doors, probably too heavy for the timber supporting them. He could see that the present owner, a retired teacher, had been practicing DIY of an untrustworthy nature.

"Honestly, Sal, I beg you not to buy this place! I feel so uncomfortable about it!"

It was probably the best advice I had been given, and I ignored it.

A few days later Mum rang up to see how things were, hoping that I had dropped the idea.

"I've sold my shares from when John and I divided the house in Thackley."

"Oh, Sal! Did you have to?"

"Of course I had to. You don't think I can buy that house without selling everything I've got, do you?"

"I suppose not. You won't sell the flat until you are sure you can get the house, will you?"

"I'm not daft you know. I've had the agent out to value my flat and told him that I won't accept less than half as much again as he suggests. I've taken picturesque photos with blue sky and puffy white clouds. Estate agents always manage such dreary photos. And I've suggested the wording in the advert. He agreed it was better than his!"

"Do you think you'll get any offers asking so much?"

"We'll see. This is a very popular village with tourists."

At one stage the agent became impatient with me: "If you want to sell this place, Miss Dalglish, you'll have to put a more realistic price on it or I can't help you."

I put an advert in the Daily Telegraph. Subsequently, the agent rang to say that a judge wished to buy it as a pied a terre for his sessions in the northern courts. A local, fearing to lose a place she coveted, bought at the higher price. No one was more surprised than the agent.

Mum had done her own conveyancing for her houses so I thought I would undertake to do all the paperwork and searches for my purchase and sale myself. The difference was that Mum's solicitors on the opposing side appeared to be sympathetic old gentlemen, willing to give her a few tips on the intricacies of conveying houses. My opposition was a sharp red-haired young woman keen to trip me up and insert a delay where one could be made.

Being the selfless man that he was, Les backed me all the way. His ambition was to enable me to stand on my own feet and lead an independent life. The day we moved in we had a tenant ready to live in the Wigton flat. It wasn't long before we found a wine judge who agreed to teach me viticulture and take away all the grapes in November to make first class wine.

It had been a dry summer. Shortly after we moved in during September there was a deluge. The septic tank had not been attended to and the drains were blocked. Effluent flooded into the scullery and conservatory. We dealt with this horror and then needed to light the solid fuel boiler but smoke was coming back into the dining room. Les carefully screwed his rods together to sweep the chimney but the chimney was cracked. This was 1990 and he was eighty-four, but there was nothing he would not tackle! A local builder came to our aid. It would not be the last time we called on him.

We dowsed and found that the place had water underneath, so we re-named it "Ching", meaning, in Chinese, "a well". Later it appeared that it could also signify a stagnant well.

With enthusiasm, I planted heavily fragrant roses and as I trimmed the high privet hedge, Lucky, the cat, would clamber up behind me and wade through the tops; or she would dart up a ladder and hang and tumble from rung to rung coming down. She remained my tactile angel, almost my reason for living, so that when she was run over on the double bend Les believed I would leave him. The only solution was to have another cat. Dynamite, too, was black and white, part Siamese. We constructed a playground for her of raised planks, and tubes for her to dart through, balls dangling from strings and soft toys to tickle her that she could chase. Together we all had endless fun. She was a cat who could sit on top of a door.

The year was filled transforming the garden, restoring rugs, discovering local walks, visiting people in Caldbeck, pruning and feeding the vines; but after Lucky's death, Les's family became increasingly concerned that, in order to reach a pavement, he must cross that lethal double bend. We both felt that we had been sold a shower of troubles by the vendor. The dated kitchen and bathroom we could not afford to renew, having spent what we had on repairs. It was not therefore an attractive proposition to sell, so I decided to use the property as collateral, rent it out and buy a terraced property in Carlisle with its added amenities and the two parks and river for walks. Les was game.

For seven years we gathered the grapes and enjoyed wine of the highest quality and for seven years we endured the afflictions of tenants, some of whom locked us out and filled the house with stolen goods; some of whom enthused about dying cars and left oil on every light switch in the place. One tenant, when we went to collect the rent in the flat had placed all her nude self-portraits round the main room, and she was extremely buxom. I wilted, but Les had been an illustrator for seventy years. Nothing shook him.

"Ching" was the only property we made a loss on. By 1997 the market had fallen and I lost thirty per cent, but the rental income had paid for any interest charges incurred. I would never have been eligible for a mortgage, but "Ching" enabled me to buy a house at Roseberry Road, which sold well and, in 1994, a smallholding overlooking the Solway Firth. Before releasing "Ching" we changed the name to Brackenwell and planted one hundred daffodils on the bend.

None of the house moves triggered hypomania. Les and I were both well organised, despite him enjoying chaos. I was in my element packing and stacking boxes with a key word on each label as to room destination and a brief list of contents. Wigton was the beginning of an upward spiral.

I had a companion whose wisdom I valued. He had given me a regimen I could follow. My visits to Dr Srinivassan were beneficial and I continued to take the lithium carbonate.

Chapter 23

Australia

What a wonderful ninetieth birthday Les had! Sixty friends and family mingled, with the wind blowing ties and scarves. Alex and Mum came. It was May 1996 and Carol had flown in from Australia. Doctors, vet, architect, mountaineers, farmers and builders all chatted freely to Les's other friends engaged in antique dealing and poetry.

Carol invited Mum and Al to Christmas in the Blue Mountains. They left on December 10th to avoid peak rates and were fortunate to travel with Quantas, who supplied enough legroom for Alex. There was mutual excitement and relief as they located Charles and Carol at the airport. Uppermost in Charles's mind was the court case he had brought against the Council who had been trying to destroy his airstrip and livelihood for sixteen years. There was *still* no news from the judge since the October trial. The strains of suspense were inevitable, compounded with a degree of uncertainty about the family visit. Alex was in good form:

"We've come to cheer you up, Charlie!"

"That's a role reversal, isn't it? Come on, you must listen to some of the official tape recordings of the trial."

He had spent months preparing his own case and studying the judges before personally defending himself in court. His performance was most impressive. He uncovered inconsistencies and untruths in the Council's case. The judge was both impressed and amused at Charles's comprehension and unshakeable grasp of the situation, not to say his unorthodox approach.

Charles was prepared to play the whole scene over to Mum and Alex (five days!) but alas, after a good section, which convinced them of his success, their jetlag caught up with them and they could no longer conceal their yawns.

The euphoria and laughter of the first few days was heart-warming for all of them. Mum's desire for her own car, aided and abetted by both Charles and the bank manager, added to the hilarity. They had arrived a fortnight before Christmas and were staying actually with Charles and Carol, although Mum's property was empty and had been for several months. The invitation to stay as guests had been made in May and it was very pleasant to feel wanted. It was a noble gesture. But the old law of Nature holds good: Guests, like fish, after five days stink!

Mum was trying to master her new word processor. Charles fitted it up on the dining room table and Mum thought that she was keeping herself acceptably occupied and out of the way. She wasted hours and was offered much unskilled help, and some skilled. Alex helped Charles with the Executive 7 (Lotus 3.5 litre) and proved that his *finish* improved the standard. He also helped Greg and Charles in the hangar building their shared kit plane, the Glastar. But he was sometimes at a loose end and was hooked on a computer game at which he exceeded all previous scores! This was in Robert's room beyond the sitting room.

Carol hated this machine because, Mum suspected, it lured Charles away from useful work when there was little incentive to finish. When finally she cracked, two or three days before Christmas, Mum thought it was the computer she resented. In fact, it was Mum and her word processor, which was set up just where she had grown used to seeing Charles working at all hours of the day and night putting his case together. Could she never be rid of that awful CASE? She had of course given him maximum support, but the pressures, anxiety and frustration of still no settlement, were brought home to her all over again.

All of them realised that it had been a superhuman effort to invite Mum and Alex for three or four months, much like handling unexploded bombs, without all the pressures they themselves had undergone. The guests were in a bit of a spot. So near Christmas it would be difficult to get No. 12 in Lithgow ready for occupation. In Mum's eyes the big difficulty was to tell Al that they were no longer welcome, especially since she believed it was his computer games that were the cause.

"Al, I think it's your computer games that have brought this about."

Having tried so hard to help Charles, fit in, and keep out of the way, Alex was heartbroken but he dealt with the blow. He took two Temazepam that night, nothing more, and woke up restored. By that time Carol had recovered her poise, the situation had been explained to Mum and she retreated to her bedroom with her *monster* machine.

They talked things over coolly.

"In many ways Al has put fresh heart into Charlie," they agreed.

"He did the same for Alex and his trike," Mum reassured Carol. "But I don't think it would do Al any good to stay at No. 12, which must be in a nagging state of disrepair. He never liked that place."

It was agreed that the guests would stay and everyone would try very hard to improve their image! Carol had a job with Lifeline, similar to the Samaritans, for which she was eminently suitable, and, with all the other burdens on her shoulders, bless her, she encouraged Mum to offload hers. Mum had always recognised her as a treasure and was overjoyed when they reached their silver wedding anniversary.

It could be said that Alex never put a foot wrong during this visit. His aims in coming were to make himself acceptable: a difficult task in view of recent traumatic history, which scared the pants off the family in England and transmitted itself over here. It threatened Charles's ability to cope if such a thing were to happen here. With all credit, he accepted the challenge.

Mum felt that she had been given two months release from her twenty-four-hour a day vigilance, which had lasted since her hip was replaced nearly two years earlier. They were hoping on their return to be in good shape to tackle Higher Clough with renewed vigour and greater confidence. They planned to extend themselves socially, developing new friendships recently made.

It seemed to Alex and Mum that all the recent troubles, going right back to the divorce, through the Will saga, the breakdowns and family estrangements – all had been caused basically by fear. Alex had begun to recognise and control the symptoms of a resulting "high".

They had had less experience of "lows". Whenever he was down he pulled himself up and made himself do some simple task, against his inclination. The resulting satisfaction restored his self-respect – his first aim of recovery. This technique failed after his last "high" breakdown. He overworked his right arm and was incapacitated. Chaos built up around him and he had to face the destruction resulting from the breakdown. He couldn't cope. He took an overdose.

When Mum discovered him in the morning and heard him breathing she was absolutely certain that his number was not up. When she saw how well he was being looked after in intensive care she explained that her time would be better spent preparing for his return, checking his condition day and night. David Moorhouse, Alex's psychiatric community nurse, brought his staff and between them they cleared the barn of broken furniture and general rubbish. It took all afternoon and a grand bonfire. Alex was enormously relieved when he came home that the evidence was gone.

Here in Little Hartley all was going at least as well as could be hoped, until the art classes which Carol sponsored for Alex. It was an interest they shared but Carol found little time for. Alex had seldom gone hard at it since his intensive portrait-painting era. He was never fully satisfied, though he attempted several aspects of art, including sculpture, with some success. Sometimes he felt he was an artist; Charles was convinced that he wasn't, but then Charles was a philistine as far as art was concerned.

Al had been trying to convince Charles that he was not merely a little brother to be treated with contempt; and not a wanton maniac, but a responsible citizen with as high, if not higher, standards than Charles's own. It may simply have been that his efforts exhausted him by the time the classes began. He didn't go with the idea of producing a masterpiece.

"I'm going along to take instruction." This must have been almost a first for him or any Dalglish.

He was enormously pleased when the artist invited him to accompany him later to make a local sketch. There was also a moment when someone saw the effect on his board and said, "Wow!" with appreciation. But alas, the classes fizzled out for him on the Thursday and Friday. He studied the artist's other work. His sleep pattern disintegrated.

Next morning, Saturday, he helped his nephew, Robert, move crates of wine and was talking with him and Carol when he just switched off in the middle, acting inconsequentially. He wandered round lost, unable to bear the noise of Robert's videos – or the contents! He suffered from introspection, some of which Mum tried to share and some he shared with Robert, who seemed to be able to "take it" and was helpful. In the evening he seized the opportunity to wash up with Carol to escape the video player and talk with her. Charles, in spite of his many great kindnesses, did not have an inkling of what was going on in Alex's mind or what was needed to resolve the situation. He was worried when Carol and Alex went off for a walk. Mum's anxiety was that he would scar Alex with his own fears! Luckily, as the pair returned, everyone was able to behave nonchalantly.

This potentially explosive situation was resolved, as far as the family at Little Hartley was concerned, by Mum and Alex going north to Charles's farm at Ulan. The journey was daunting: three and a half hours by road - a long enough drive for anyone, but for one completely exhausted who hated to let anyone else drive, it was almost too much. First, they had to stop at Lithgow to give the real estate agent, Sue, duplicate keys for the prospective tenant who had agreed to pay Mum $120 a week. Next, they went to the bank to extract $500 holiday money, only to find out the supply was exhausted. However, Mum convinced the manager that rental income was coming in again and he obliged.

They took the journey leisurely, Alex clearly losing steam, stopping several times: once at Pearson's Lookout to take photos and other places by the roadside, mostly in the shade. It was growing significantly hotter the further north they travelled. By the time they reached Running Stream they decided to lunch at the Cherry Tree where Charles and Carol had taken them when demonstrating a car to a possible buyer.

It was not only a tasty little meal, but they found that they could stock up with most things to sustain life for a few days. It saved the necessity of shopping in Mudgee. Alex was sharp enough to notice two "slips" at the cash register and joked over them, but made no fuss.

He drove the next short stint and let Mum take over. Tea on arrival, and a not too devastatingly hot day, mercifully. Alex looked for the new radio in the lounge: unable to find it he was not too bothered.

His energy was flagging. They sat around and Mum tried to impart a few positive thoughts. Dodgy ground! The reason for this depression could have been exhaustion from best behaviour, Charles's unsympathetic comments or the bad timing of the art classes. He had hoped to establish credibility in Charles's eyes as an artist. But even if he had, Charles's contempt for art and artists would have been unscathed.

"It's not a proper job. It's nothing. Alex isn't an artist anyway. It's your fault! You've been feeding him this rubbish all these years. He ought to have been kicked up the backside years ago and made to go out and get a living like everyone else."

"Oh, Charles! May you be forgiven!"

Mum believed that she was a tower of strength but Charles ruthlessly depicted her as the laughing stock of the family with her rose-coloured glasses and irrepressible optimism.

"You're too powerful, Mum. You're responsible for all the family ills. You've robbed Alex of a normal man's life and a chance of finding a wife. You've overindulged him."

Cut to the quick Mum could only respond, "Can one ever see oneself as others see us?"

His remarks rankled with her long after the return to England, the jet lag, flu and depression.

Talking was not lifting Alex out of his despair so Mum rang the local medical team. The hospital put her through to the Community Health Centre where she asked to speak to someone who knew something about manic-depression. The girl didn't know but promised to find someone to phone back. An hour later Mum rang again. It was a different girl.

"Listen! We are fighting a suicide here! There is some urgency!"

Complete panic! The phone was dropped like a hot brick. There was a long pause. Then a calm voice asked, "Can I help you?"

"Ah!" Mum said with relief. "I very much hope you can!"

It was Julie Blamire who happened to be passing the desk and noticed the dangling phone. She had picked it up out of curiosity. She was exactly the person they needed. She cancelled her plans to receive them as soon as they could get there. Alex had rallied at the thought of a nice helpful girl and shaved! A good sign, which she appreciated.

Julie assessed Alex then called Mum in: they had spoken copiously over the phone. She had nearly persuaded Alex to go into hospital, which Mum considered a backward step, so she sent them on to Dr McKendry.

They worked well together, both excellent in manner and approach and each of them agreeing that suicidal tendencies were not evident. Dr McKendry could prescribe nothing until he could contact the elusive David Horsfield in England. They had heard no news on Thursday or Friday. On Thursday, Mum tried what she called her "jump lead" treatment, whereby they both flaked out on the bed holding hands while Mum exhorted him to take fresh hope and let go of all the absurd self-recriminations.

On Saturday, hearing that neither of their two new friends would be about till Monday, Mum first rang the duty doctor who said that Largactil could do no harm, and then the pharmacist who prescribed Largactil.

Sunday was a new day. They would venture out to see the neighbours, Owen and Olive. First, Alex wanted to go out for a little walk, hat on, but without a shirt, to let the sun get to his back, which was becoming greasy in the heat and pimply. Not too much sun; just a little walk, first thing. Another time, a longer one. But it was getting late when he started and he went as far as the railway line, the longer walk.

On his return there was rather too much deep introspection and a faraway look.

"Do you think it might be a good idea to take some Largactil? How about it?" Mum suggested.

"No, Mum, I'm going to be all right without that."

No good pushing, but Mum had found both 50mg and 100mg in the bathroom, which was fortuitous, because, after sitting in the doorway in the breeze with a vacant stare, Alex suddenly rolled his eyes upwards in a look of terror yelling: "Doctor! Get the Doctor! Quick!" The Largactil (200mg) were at hand.

What caused the panic Mum had no idea. One thing was absolutely clear: there was no chance of medical help in less than twenty-four hours. Recalling the duty doctor's assurance that Largactil could do no harm, Mum resorted to this medication, having no experience of sunstroke or how to deal with it. She comforted him as best she could, gave him Largactil, put pillows under his head where he had fallen prostrate in the bathroom, head inches short of the loo, feet leaving clearance for the door. She kept up a steady stream of wet flannels to the head and tepid sponging to body and limbs, which he acknowledged gratefully before going off to sleep at about 3.00pm. He was still asleep at 6.30pm. Mum hoped that when he awoke for a drink and two Temazepam later, the normal routine would be restored.

Charles rang to say that they had not had too good a time at the airshow due to atrocious weather. They were lucky to get out when they did.

Alex woke at 11.00pm and was pretty lucid by 12.30am, although he was unclear about what had happened. Mum told him she'd given him two Largactil pills and that they seemed to have done him good.

"If I bring you one now, would you take it?"

"Most certainly I would!" was his astonishing answer. Usually, when taking Largactil appears to be the right answer, it meets with huge reluctance. Alex might concede to half what was prescribed. Mum found over the years that timing was essential. The moment, once missed, the chance was gone. They had had greater success controlling the "highs" but little practice over "lows". It was confirmed in Dubbo that too high a dose could do no harm, but Mum knew from experience that not enough could spell disaster. She gave him another 200mg. He surfaced happily in the morning with, "I never felt better in my life!"

"Hoorah!" Mum cried out, too soon.

Alex became psychotic again, going into spasm, gurgling uncomfortably and throwing his head back. There were fewer spells of lucidity. As the day warmed up he sweated and Mum tried to keep him cool by constant cold sponging and changing the cold flannel on his brow. Mostly, he liked no bedclothes or anything else except his pants, but sometimes the sheet, used as a fan gave him comfort.

He enjoyed a milo milkshake from the fridge (after the midnight Largactil) – the last before the ice cream finally liquefied. The gas had run out, so no more fridge, no more cooking and no hot water. Mum couldn't leave it to Alex to explore for another cylinder but later Carol told her where to find one, and when she had the chance, when he appeared to be sleeping normally, she hauled one up. With her feeble wrists and uncertainty of thread direction, she was unable to do the swap over.

At 9.00am on Monday, Mum rang Julie to say that they were unlikely to be able to come in for the appointment at 2.30pm at the Health Centre. At 12.50pm, knowing that to keep the appointment which included the psychiatrist, they would have to set off at 1.15, Julie rang to check, hoping against hope that they could make it, but adding that it might still be possible to send someone to collect Alex if she couldn't get him into the car.

In the end the appointment was missed. Julie and the nurse who worked with her came out. The nurse vaguely knew the district, but, thinking that no one had lived at Redhills (names mean nothing in the outback) for twenty years, she missed the double gates and track over the railway.

Alex was eventually picked up and taken into hospital where Julie explained that Largactil and sunstroke were a disastrous combination. He was nursed sweetly back to normality, and he and Mum returned to the less searing heat of Little Hartley. In trying to ward off his "suicide" she had nearly murdered him.

Charles and Carol's airshow guests had gone and Alex was able to get out his pastels and draw humorous takes on Australian birds, one for each member of the family. He and Robert spent a few days on Hamilton Island where parakeets and cockatoos flocked to be fed from Alex's hands on the balcony. At Little Hartley he carved a memorable stone sculpture for Carol's garden. Faye and Robert would never forget the uproarious games of cards with him when he so often caught them off their guard. All three enjoyed a game of French cricket. Charles was less acutely offensive. His world would always revolve round his inventions and aircraft.

Chapter 24

The Broads

On return from Australia, Alex had actually been positive in outlook. Mum felt that this was triumph at last, expected by her. The dream was renewed and enhanced. The main objective for the summer of '97 was to be the completion of the workshop – Alex's own instinct and Charles's advice. He longed to get the structure finished from his pile of rocks and worked on the guttering, postponing the floor until the cattle grid was safe for the delivery of sand and ballast.

The cattle grid was a daunting problem involving estimates from rival firms. The size of these precluded them all! In the end he devised a simple remedy and his new friend, Adrian, from the Resource Centre volunteered to help with welding. This involved some five hours' work on a Sunday afternoon.

Both of them were naturally tired and, over supper, Adrian began telling them of his tragic life. He was almost friendless and without root, his wife having died recently of cancer. Neither had any family at all. His jobs had taken him all over the country and to an oilrig. While it was wonderful to make new friends and be able to help anyone in such a position, the emotional burden coming after physical hard labour at such a time, was pretty testing. Mum had to suggest at ten o'clock when Alex was obviously wilting, that sleep was important.

Adrian admitted with a laugh, "I very often don't feel like going to bed till three o'clock in the morning."

The simple thing might have been to offer him a bed at Higher Clough, but Mum did not feel it was that simple, and might have been too much too soon. Adrian was responsive and left gracefully. They met again at the

Resource Centre where Adrian offered to help with concreting the floor.

The satisfaction of strengthening the cattle grid was tremendous but Alex did not go on to order sand and ballast. He worked on his social life, intending to work with Burt on fibre glassing his boat in exchange for help with his moped. He had also hoped to become involved in sailing and attend TT races. The trike too needed a major overhaul.

For a couple of years Alex had got around by using Mum's car, often leaving her grounded. Why not take the moped to a garage and have it fixed? It would cost money, and why spend money on a job he could have done himself in better days? The aim when they came to Higher Clough was to re-establish Alex's self-esteem. He was the master of the house, thus it was he who decided what should be done.

The weeks passed and Alex put off work on the workshop in favour of gardening. He avoided deciding where the stop tap should go, in or outside the workshop and greenhouse. His brain was tired. Mum suggested that she would like the use of her car, "If you use your moped to go to the pottery classes, I could bring Doris over to see the garden."

Immediately he rang Burt and arranged for him to come to lunch next day and pick up the moped, explaining that it was somewhat urgent. Burt obligingly agreed but telephoned some hours after his expected arrival just when David Horsfield was expecting Dr Kenny to see Alex. Mum cursed herself for bringing the transport subject up at a tactless moment.

When David came after the long weekend and they had an unhurried talk in the Summer House, Alex was not well. He was mostly silent while Mum spoke freely to David. Why? Why was he more silent in response to David than to Mum? Was he too tired to talk? Was it remonstrance that David was not available when he needed him?

Dr Burrows would recall what happened when she first interviewed Alex. He was silent after giving particulars to Brenda whom he knew. Dr Burrows and Mum exchanged pleasantries. She turned to Alex who remained silent. The phone rang. Dr Burrows answered it. There followed a conversation, brief but inconsequential as far as Alex was concerned. He emerged from his silence and, sitting forward on his chair, declared to Dr Burrows: "Stop! Don't say any more!" His voice was authoritative, like the time he made the Garage sell Mum a car they had already sold to someone else. Totally out of character.

"Don't say another word!" Alex repeated. Dr Burrows rang off and turned her attention to Alex, who had nothing more to say.

Dr Burrows apologised, "I'm sorry about that – it was nothing to do with Alex."

"That was the point," Mum defended him. "He has come to see you. He doesn't know you. To him *his* case is of the utmost importance and you are sidetracked. It was bad enough when I digressed with you about Dr MacKenzie."

Dr Burrows sensibly retreated and fetched Judith, who, David had told them outside, remembered Alex.

Alex arrived at Airedale Hospital expecting to be seen by the doctor to whom David had spoken on the phone on other occasions. This sort of thing was reassuring to a patient who was naturally scared stiff of committing himself to return to a place from which he has been, for far too long, unable to escape. To be interviewed by another doctor was a comedown. Alex was naturally reluctant to say anything, feeling that he was not in control of what he said and knowing that he might easily be misunderstood, as when he gave an ambiguous answer to the question: "Do you hear voices?"

Talking to Mum later he said he might have given the wrong answer. He'd never actually heard a voice in his mind but had been extremely worried when Simon had told him that *he* had.

Mum had noticed that the "switch off" periods inevitably followed periods of over-taxing. It took very little to over-tax him: a short conversation; a meal, a walk, a bath. He seemed to know his limits up to a point. If he went too far, he would collapse. His symptoms seemed to suggest complete exhaustion. Now that he had settled for a complete rest in hospital, Mum was convinced that he would recover in his own time and in his own way.

He recovered his strength in hospital. Adrian was waiting to help him finish the workshop and the fibre glassing of the trike when he came home. Sunny days were encouraging, but there were clashes in the fact that Alex preferred to work from 9.00am until 5.00pm where Adrian would not appear till 1.00pm without some persuasion and would want to work on till 7.00pm.

"You both need a holiday!" Adrian exclaimed one day. "Let's go to the Broads. It would be very peaceful. Leave it to me. I'll organise this."

By the time they set off for the Broads there was a minimal amount to do to complete work on the trike and the workshop. Alex showed signs of fatigue and dissatisfaction, but then his standards were always astronomically high. The trike passed its MOT. Mum could only say: "Success! Triumph!" But Alex felt no elation. Had he no joy in riding it any more?

He had anxieties about the mooring challenges they were going to face on the long boat and the idea of moving into completely unknown territory. A week on water would not have seemed a boring prospect to him had it been the nesting season. To compensate, it would offer a change of scene with minimal effort. There would be people around to provide superficial social background. And there would be Adrian. For it was a highly desirable prospect bringing back a whole world of happy memories, not otherwise retraceable. He promised to provide all the enthusiasm, energy, organisation, efficiency and effort to allow Mum and Alex a complete rest. His obvious longing to revisit old haunts was an added incentive to them; by going, even if they put all the weight on his shoulders, they would be doing him a good turn.

Apprehension had been mounting with Alex's shrinking sense of achievement. They could have cancelled the trip, but Mum had come to see it as her first chance in two years to come off Red Alert twenty-four hours a day seven days a week. With such a prospect she had begun to crack and become impatient. No longer could she recognise the signs of panic/exhaustion and insist on rest/reassurance spells each day. She began to react by, "Why on earth can't he *see* that he has won his battle and be all set to rejoice?"

It irked her more and more. Gone was her limitless supply of faith and energy. She insisted on taking a complete holiday herself, leaving Alex to cope as best he could (which was really very well!) and Adrian to do almost all the work. Alex did help him with the navigation and survived splendidly except for one horrific moment, while moored in the middle of nowhere, he seemed suddenly to have reached "switch-off" point. Mum mirrored his panic. Diazepam might have helped. They'd taken trouble to get David to get hold of some before he went out. They'd worked well once before; but they'd been left behind.

They were left with the choice of Olanzapine, as yet untried, and Zimovane, which would beget sleep and upset the sleep pattern. All three discussed the situation and Mum and Alex lay down to rest: he was soon back to normal, the built in blessing of panics. He made such a remarkable steady recovery that Mum once more was crowing to herself, "He's out of the woods!" aware that Alex did not see things the way she did. It puzzled her that there was such an interminable gulf between her faith and his lack of it. After all these years of trying to reinforce his, she felt that hers was crumbling.

The more convinced Mum was that Alex was overcoming his challenges triumphantly and was on his way to controlling his life on a permanently secure and more enriching basis than ever before, the more he shrank in terror. Perhaps, because she kept mentioning her conviction. He seemed to find her power of optimism overwhelming and her quest for spirituality annihilating. Where she saw salvation and the happy ending of their struggle, he saw only the tidal wave of her joy and felt submerged. She could admit that she had a tendency to rejoice too soon.

She tried to get him to read innumerable "positive" books: all anathema to him. Sometimes she would see the dead look of despair on his face and feel desperately that he was trying to destroy himself. Her reaction, to try and introduce hope, seemed only to make matters worse. Art was a subject they could not discuss because, by her own admission, Mum knew nothing about it and the slightest criticism invoked distress. And yet it was Alex's repressed passion.

Awaiting them, on their return from the holiday on 12th September, was a book on Stress. Alex read a few pages and put it aside. Mum was still wondering why he allowed himself to give up, and tried to check her own thoughts of triumph, which always seemed to be so short-lived. They had always talked easily every day until Mum gave her usual cheerful admonition as they said "goodnight" on Saturday.

"Don't! Mum! Don't tell me we've had a good day and it's going to be even better tomorrow! It's rubbish! I don't want to hear."

There was nothing to lose: "Look, Al, your attitude is destroying us both! Sometimes I want to scream! You're so wrapped up in yourself you don't notice what's happening to me!"

"I'm sorry, Mum, but the more you cheer me on the worse I feel. I'll try and change."

His ambition was to drop regular medication. To this end they reduced the Olanzapine gradually from 15mg to 7.5mg each night. Initially, he awoke restless and "scattered" and cold. As the days went by he recovered but still lacked energy. He looked really tired but over the winter he and Adrian made small inroads into the work to be done and he faithfully fed all his birds, even the pheasants that called.

Chapter 25

Where is the Car?

Stan's death and not long after, the death of Elsie, rendered Alex desolate. He had spent so many hours laughing and chatting with each of these dear old friends over the years. He refused to cry but his grief was enervating. He and Mum set about the garden, concentrating on the edging. They made plans for the future: to try and tidy up Higher Clough for sale, with or without help. Some moments Alex appeared to be more confidant and positive than others. After a brew Mum went off to busy herself with lunch. When she looked round, the black mood was on him again and he said firmly that he meant to end it all. These moods descended sometimes but were not usually so intense and didn't last long. A little inconsequential chatter would usually disperse the mood. This one was unexpected. Was the prospect too overwhelming? This surely was the moment to call Dr Kenny! Now they could really get together. All Alex needed was reassurance. Dr Kenny's very presence as an ordinary man with common sense and compassion was welcome. He said just the right thing reminding Alex that he had lived for eight years without medication. He could do it again! That was exactly what Alex needed to hear – from him, as well as Mum. He was happy again, laughing as Dr Kenny returned for his forgotten bag.

For some time now Mum's head had been bursting, her patience exhausted, and her faith almost extinguished. Did no one realise that the sickening optimism of hers was merely a cloak for her own fears? She tried never to show fear, thinking it unhelpful. Did no one realise that for thirty years she had been concerned for the special needs of her family, and that for twelve years, since the first attempt at suicide heralding Alex's breakdown, she had lived in its shadow ever since? For the last few years she had never dared to leave him alone.

"I have no one in whom I can confide who would understand at all what I am on about."

Certainly she had always protected me from knowing about Alex's incarcerations in Airedale Hospital or continual state of vulnerability. He only visited Les and me when he felt fairly confident and could smile and laugh and recount tales of progress. They came to see us one April and called briefly on Dr Bob, whose hearty greeting, sympathy and common sense were enough in themselves to restore health! Mum found it restorative to be treated as a friend rather than chief suspect.

In Australia they had treated Alex's exhaustion and said he was not suicidal. In Lancashire David and Dr MacKenzie tended to go into a flat spin and want to increase the drugs. Dr MacKenzie even put Alex on a Section 3, which resulted in terror and a broken window. No bird likes to be caged.

Simon had managed his "Spring fever" very well from the 1970s when Dr Morrissey put him on Valium. He mostly avoided hospital and for twenty years avoided contact with me in case my touches of hypomania triggered anything similar in him. More recently he has been prescribed lithium carbonate.

There was an outstanding appointment at the hospital that Alex did not want to attend. Nor did he want David dropping in unexpectedly. As luck would have it he met David in the bank. They spoke cheerfully and Alex cancelled the appointment with Dr Blake at the end of the month.

Alex and Adrian happily spent an afternoon sawing and chopping up a surplus eucalyptus tree. Mum was feeling inside herself: "Now it really is: all stations go! Alex is reducing his tablets. Soon he will recover his confidence and energy, and then – Look out!"

Only a few days later she was kicking herself for not being more aware. Alex had not been sleeping well for some nights. At least he had no further indigestion. Nausea had been troubling him previously. He wasn't upset by the lack of sleep and had begun to read a book. Progress? Too late: he began to talk of ending it all again. They tried whatever drugs they had available from Zimovane to Mogadon and even some of Dandan's old sleeping tablets. Mum was getting frightened.

She rang the surgery on Thursday.

"Dr Kenny's gone on holiday. Would anyone else do?"

When Alex next mentioned ending it all, Mum said, laughingly, "Well, it's no good trying pills again. There aren't enough in the house, and you'd only end up in hospital."

He promised he would not and spent the day idly, laying the fire; going for the paper while Mum made scones. They played bezique together and watched snooker by the fire.

He went out to the workshop. After ten minutes Mum went out to the workshop but there was no one there. She went up to the Summerhouse and was just coming down the steps when she heard him call. He was the other side of the front door. But where was his car?

They greeted each other with a laugh and a hug.

"What have you done with your car?"

"Oh, I've put it somewhere. Up there," he said with a smile heading for the house. No point making issues. Later, with a torch, thinking to remove they keys, she looked up and down the lane, but didn't see it. The gate was shut at the top. She took her own car keys out and, having seen him asleep with an extra couple of Zimovane and water in case he woke, Mum threw a duvet over herself in the kitchen, on guard. It was 4.00am.

"Oh God! – How long?" Mum wondered. "Can he be sleeping peacefully? Can the darned pills be taking effect at last?"

It was his confidence which, despite all his huge efforts and Mum's, that needed restoring. "And if he can't believe any longer in our team, or in my ability to help him, and he can't believe in himself, or anything at all, how can he live? And how can pills help?"

She pondered his last words to her as he went through the door: "You've pushed me too hard, Mum. I can't live up to your standards."

He was mistaken: she couldn't reach *his* standards. Why else would he not let her join in the building or even the housework in his dream house?

While she was keeping watch in the kitchen, thinking that even if he bypassed it he'd have to go through the dining room and out through the barn and couldn't possibly open those doors without rousing her – he went out through the sitting room window.

She thought of checking him many times during the night. But there was their mutual trust to observe. Was it already broken? If she went up and he was asleep, she would surely wake him. Should he wake early, just how early? Would he take the extra Zimovane? If he did take the extra, how long would they last? Not till the normal 8.00pm, surely? She went in at 7.00pm. His bed was empty. She shrank. Her body felt cold. She could feel her heart beating.

Where was his car? She went over to the cattle grid in her bedroom slippers. No car. The gate at the top was shut. Still? Or again? There was a tyre mark showing that the car had been through the gate. Where could he have gone? What was his plan? What could he do? He'd spoken of going south again. Had he decided to try that? Could he make it on his own in his present state of energy? Had he gone off to find a place to die? Had he found enough pills somehow to do the job? Mum had warned him that it was not worth it since there were not enough for his purpose and he'd end up in hospital again. The whole purpose of his life lately had been to avoid hospital. What else could he have done? And where had he done it?

She alerted the police: first Clitheroe who came out and realised that they were in the Barnoldswick area, which had to be contacted through Colne. They asked for car details. People are endlessly kind under such circumstances. Mum could describe Alex's old Volvo, but not the number. She phoned Adrian about the logbook. Every other vehicle he'd ever had was documented, but not the Volvo. She rang the police at intervals suggesting possible lines of enquiry: the M6, Greenberfield Locks; the old Gisburn track. Was it 10.00am when she rang to ask if anything had been heard? There was some hesitation, and at the same time a flurry at the door and a running figure.

She went to the door and eventually caught up with a young policewoman who asked, "Can I use the phone? My radio doesn't work in this area." She rang for an ambulance.

"Have you found him? Where is he?" Mum couldn't understand what was going on.

"He's here!"

"Where?"

"Just up there!"

He'd been within yards of Mum all this time. His car was still in the field, beyond the scope of Mum's bedroom slippers and out of sight behind the high shrubbery wall.

"He's alive?"

"Yes."

And all this time she had been compounding his efforts. Within a stone's throw he was continuing his deadly intention. What irony! After his last effort, when he barricaded himself into his room and took an overdose – once Mum heard him breathing she knew that his number was not up. He revived from that episode cheerfully. Now there was no such certainty of the future. He had switched on the engine and lain under the exhaust for who knows how many hours?

I phoned just as the ambulance was arriving. Mum explained what had happened. I was shocked for Alex, who had hidden his distress so well from us and for Mum, "You shouldn't have tried to carry this burden on your own, Mum! You should have told us what was going on. How can we know if you don't tell us? I'm coming down to see him. I'm coming down to see you, Mum!"

Alex had maintained for weeks: "If I go into hospital, I shall never come out again."

Mum kept assuring him that no hospital could keep him indefinitely. He was convinced that she was wrong.

"Why think of such a possibility anyway? You're so nearly out of your pit. I've watched your progress this last nine months. I've seen you gathering strength and confidence."

Alex was caught in the crossfire between two philosophies. As Dr Kenny had suggested to Mum, "He is, as it were, a stoated rabbit!"

His catatonic body was taken first to Airedale Hospital and afterwards to Burnley Intensive Care Unit, since he was not fit to be cared for in a psychiatric ward. On 1st May he was still catatonic. Occasionally, he looked peaceful and slept. Sometimes he badly wanted to speak. It was distressing all round not to be able to understand. All week he was on antibiotics for fever and fed glucose by drip feed. On the Tuesday an Indian woman doctor told Mum that he had Nerve Malignant Syndrome. Not understanding immediately she asked if he was going to recover and she shook her head. Mum got the impression that he was likely to get no better, but to be uncertain to die.

That was the worst moment. Mum said that she was tempted to help him and that she had always promised...the doctor said no more. It was only later that the name rang a bell. Mum went to the desk to ask if that were the same condition brought about by Largactil and sunstroke. It was.

Then surely there was hope that it would right itself? The nurse didn't seem to be very sure. Perhaps they were psychiatric drugs with which she was not very familiar. Anyway, Mum's hopes rose, as they always did on the smallest speculation! It was just a matter of waiting for the blood pressure and so on to come down, as they had explained in Australia. Next morning they started to do just that. In Intensive Care it was quiet and spacious. Burnley had a high reputation. The staff's care of both Mum and Alex was first class.

On Friday he seemed to be making slight progress when Mum arrived at 9.00am. He seemed to smile, or at least convey pleasure. While Mum was off the ward, two nurses heard him say, "Hospital. Brakes off." Was the latter the result of the muscle relaxant? Blood pressure, temperature and pulse were coming down steadily and Mum assumed that the danger was passed. But the Indian doctor said, "There is an enzyme still causing trouble."

Mum took Min in on Friday evening, hoping he would really be talking by then. But he had been moved back into Ward 1 and when they saw him he was back in his shell and seemed to have gone downhill a little. Min was very pale and far from her ebullient self. She was profoundly upset. Mum wondered whether *she* had been taking the situation too lightheartedly altogether.

At least he had not gone into a psychiatric ward: neurological, quite different. Perhaps he was tired after all these moves? Mum's heavy heart next day was comforted by Radio 4's thought for the day that "all will be well" and by meeting a nurse, Debbie who assured Mum that Alex was in good form on arrival and "we've 'ad lots of laffs". Mum realised that Alex would be more in his element now, remembering King Edward VII hospital days.

Mum felt that there was no need for her to hover over him when he was better off in the company of these cheerful young nurses.

"He's a handsome lad," Debbie said. "It's nice to see he has a sense of humour."

Mum loitered by the door for Debbie's return, but she was busy. In the end Mum told an African nurse that she would be visiting less. "But please call me if he shows signs of wanting to see me."

Chapter 26

The Hospice

"Now for the garden!" Mum, a sprightly eighty-two-year old vowed, convinced that faith and a bent fork could move mountains. Alex, surely, would never have to face a Section 3 again and this would speed a hasty recovery.

I came to see him in Burnley Hospital. He was on Warfarin to prevent blood clots. Didn't we kill the rats with that at John Peel's cottage? Dear Alex, who had always been my protector in the Sussex days, especially when I was studying weaving. I kissed him on the temple. He was naked in the bed, the sheets falling away from him. I straightened the covers. What an actor! He had always shown me his good side: his strength, his great sense of humour. The image suddenly crossed my mind of a Black Widow Spider who wrapped her mate in silk and consumed him. Had Mum's overpowering optimism sapped Alex's will to live? I laid my head against his face and hugged his shoulders and then I knew, it was no good, I would have to go; I was only going to cry and never stop.

Alex could cry and laugh but not speak or feed or cleanse himself. And still Mum was convinced that his nerves would grow in time. She would exhort him at his bedside: "You have shown great courage and you have overcome huge challenges in life. You have fulfilled and part-fulfilled colossal dreams. And there is much to be done.

"You have pushed yourself further than anyone else ever did and you have faced almost total misunderstanding, but you are greatly loved and valued, and possibly becoming more widely understood by those you love. Simon has found his gift for healing in Reiki and is developing it especially in order to help you. Sal is beginning to learn patience and tolerance. Her understanding is widening.

"My own trust, which I shared with you for so many years, which was devastated by your rejection, is recovering happily when you seem pleased to see me. Something is achieved each day when we read stories, when you laugh or down a beaker of liquid. It is like mountaineering. Slow-going. The valleys are deep but the mountain is waiting to be climbed. So we must brace ourselves for the climb. You know how we did it at the outset. The main aim was to regain your self-esteem, self-control, independence…"

And so she battled with encouragement. When two members of staff spoke about him in front of him, the tears would trickle out of his cornflower blue eyes. It was obvious he could hear but utter nothing. How could he escape or respond to Mum's homily?

Daily in her visits she would recount his challenges and achievements: "Do you remember the hours you spent rain-pointing every stone in the three stories of Higher Clough? No builder ever took so much trouble."

At other times she might sound a little patronising, "Don't forget, my dear, that we always have a choice. We can be grumpy or we can be cheerful for a start! To be grumpy smacks of selfishness – self-pity – and it takes the smile off other people's faces when they are trying to be cheerful.

"Then you have to remember that if you are fed up with the present circumstances you have to look around for what you want to change. Don't give yourself the quick answer, 'I can't.' Go on thinking about it until you can see some glimmer of hope. It may seem impossible at first. But keep working at it.

"Everything starts in the mind. Nothing you ever did just happened. It started as an idea, a dream and became a reality. You've done quite a lot of this in your time. Don't stop now!

"It is more difficult now, I know, because your body does not leap into response as it used to do. But it is still working. All the essential functions keep going, though some need a bit of a boost. Your heart is strong, your lungs, your digestion and, up to a point, your limbs. The automatic pilot keeps going. But it is your Will that has taken the biggest battering, and that is most closely allied with your spirit.

"It is the spirit that governs what we do with our lives and our will that distinguishes us as individuals. If we can believe in a Universal Spirit…"

"Would you like a cup of tea, Mrs Dalglish?" a bright young nurse enquired.

Alex had turned his head away.

"Alex," she smiled. "Shall I give you this beaker?" He smiled back. "Or do you want your Mum to hold it?" He lowered his eyes. Mum gave it to him, sip by sip.

As the days passed Mum detected positive traces of encouragement.

"Hello Al, I wonder if we hit on something good yesterday, which may lead to something better! Do you remember we made up sentences and you repeated them quite clearly and easily?

"Yet when you produce your own sentences I too often miss the chief word which would make sense of the others. We could try repeating sentences that you can say and I can hear and understand. But it will be no use doing it 'parrot fashion'. We'll have to find out why you know what you mean to say but I can't understand it, and why you can say what I want to hear, but you can't make sense of that.

"We know fatigue and exhaustion are the root of your troubles, but you are still very much alive and the natural process of fatigue is rest and recovery."

I had explained to Mum what I had heard from a Naturopath that Alex's nerve endings, being burnt out living tissue, need desperately to regrow before the messages of instruction could get through.

By November, Sister was concerned that Alex was becoming a long-term patient in a hospital: "This fog of uncertainty is destroying him. We can't provide any stimulus for him and it takes three nurses to lift him." She laughed at Mum's idea of taking him home. All Mum's enquiries had met with silence or evasion. No exception was the DLA.

Finally, a place was found for him at St. Andrews Home for Adults, Barnoldswick. I was shocked to find so many contorted faces and disfigured limbs, but the atmosphere was one of kindliness and happiness and all the staff were cheerful and friendly.

In Alex's room we set up a CD player so that as often as a passer-by could change it, he could listen to his favourite Chopin or Tchaikovsky. He looked forward to sessions with the physiotherapist and would smile and laugh with her. The man in charge would lay a grey fluffy rug on his head saying, "Look, young Alex, we're going to have to give you a haircut!"

Al's blue eyes would twinkle.

But I looked at the end of his bed and saw the stream of medication he was on for alleged: schizophrenia, mania, depression…you name it, he had a drug for it.

"He's never going to sit up and hit you with a damp flannel! Does he have to have all this medication?" I asked. "Could I give him St. John's Wort to soothe any depression he might have?"

"He's not written up for it. We can't go giving alternative medicine."

He continued with a tube into his stomach for feeding, enemas and a catheter. Mum might feed him a few sips of fruit yoghurt. I brought him a platypus with a tube for sipping water if he ever felt hot. A platypus on my back was a great refresher when I was walking up and down the fells in the Lake District. I came one day to find to my chagrin that Mum had filled it with orange juice, making it indistinguishable from his catheter tube. It would also rapidly develop bacteria, so I threw it out.

When I could no longer do twenty-four hour a day care for Les, he went to the Caldbeck Residential Home where all his medical friends and family visited him. He liked interesting people around him and never lost his curiosity or powers of observation.

Initially, I moved into a cottage that had been lovingly restored by the previous owner who used only doweling pegs for the battened doors, not a screw in sight. The coal fire was welcoming. It was one of the homeliest places I have lived in, with lots of visitors and plenty of fun to be had with surrounding neighbours. I took up photography and massage and regularly called on Les or phoned.

However, as soon as Les died in 2000, I made arrangements to sell Sparrow Hill, and found a holiday cottage, no longer wanted, in Gargrave, which would enable me to visit Alex at the hospice and thereby reduce the frequency of Mum's visits. I tended to stroke his hair or pat his arms to release static electricity; hum a bit of the Chopin Nocturne or listen while he said earnestly: "Do, do, do, do, do, do."

"I will, Alex, I will. I will," I reassured him quietly, not at that time sure whether I was going to justify his existence, draw attention to his art, which Mum had not understood or do something for him that might express that free bird-like spirit that so loved birds and had got so ensnared that he had no longer felt like flying.

Communication between an emotional, creative free spirit and an intellectual philosopher had reached an impasse. I searched my own avenues for help. It appeared that stem cells could be cultivated and somehow surgically inserted in the brain to aid restoration of the damaged area. I didn't get a signal that this was what Alex wanted.

Funding for the hospice had involved much negotiation. The DSS would contribute nothing until all Alex's own funds were exhausted – everything bar the house, which would be taken later. Mum wanted to do something for St. Andrews in gratitude for all the care and kindness they had shown. Between them, with suggestions and nods, they decided to buy a secondhand Mercedes passenger carrier that could be adapted to transport several wheelchairs. Alex's hopes were raised that he might be driven up to Higher Clough.

Alex was aware when the Mercedes arrived. He was distressed when other people were taken out in it but not him: to such an extent that he developed two gastric ulcers. He was taken to Burnley Hospital where Mum and I continued to visit him. He was there with the same drips and paraphernalia Dad had during his last weeks in hospital. We were approached about the possibility of an operation at Easter. To remove the ulcers was a delicate operation. He might not survive. Mum was in favour of going ahead.

"What about all the theatre staff and surgeons? How are they going to feel if he dies on the operating table? It will always be on their consciences. The operation is not going to alter his condition significantly," I volunteered.

We declined the operation. In hindsight Mum may have been right.

"Have you got a ten-second morphine drip?" I asked, knowing Les had been given one for his final hours at Caldbeck.

"What! In Burnley? In this hospital? We'll try and get one from another hospital."

Mum and I came in early one morning to hear a man screaming as the gastric ulcers perforated and released acid throughout his body.

At the nurses' station one said to the other: "I do wish that cabbage would stop screamin'. He's wakin' all the other patients!"

Alex had always been so quietly spoken and considerate when well. The comment that pierced me was my only indictment of the nursing staff's impeccable care.

Simon asked the driver of the hearse: "How fast does this thing go?"

"A hundred miles an hour, sir."

"Put your foot on it between Barnoldswick and Skipton." Alex loved speed. The cortege would be made up of TVRs and Lotus Sevens.

Chapter 27

Property

Packing and moving houses was one of my strengths, but I was not welcome at Higher Clough where Simon removed all Alex's resources and family furniture to Admergill Hall. Mum was given a caravan to live in outside the barn. Alex had left no Will. His home was sold at half its value to a nearby prosperous builder. The Inland Revenue seemed likely to take half of the proceeds.

Several of my friends in Carlisle expressed similar thoughts: "If your family don't want you, come back to Carlisle. We're your family here."

The man who had restored my Burgh Road cottage so sympathetically found me a four-bedroomed 1930's semi in Beechwood Avenue, which the selling price of the Gargrave terraced house enabled me to buy. He later steered me towards a Victorian house, which he coveted but could not afford. Together we dug and stocked a pond. My old friend, Catherine, enticed me down to Armathwaite where she found the people so congenial.

Three years after my return to Carlisle, I was introduced by a "like-minded" group, to John, a medium of high repute. He took my hand and held up his palm.

"I have here in my palm a dove. All the pain, all the anguish is gone. He thanks you for all you tried to do. He and your father were your guardian angels. It is almost unheard of for guardian angels to be present and alive at the same time as those they watch over. They both loved birds. They both needed their freedom."

I was shaken and moved to tears.

My burden, the mental disorder, has made of me a rolling boulder, rolling in and out of hospital, in and out of relationships and in and out of houses. Rarely did I live in a house for more than three years. Despite the winds from Siberia and America meeting at High Meadows, I endeavoured to plant a fragrant rose garden, a small orchard, a plantation of miniature trees and a superb vegetable patch round the old septic tank. Les helped distribute the gravel on the renovated drive. The builder constructed wind wall defenses, arches and a fountain. I was probably having as much fun and satisfaction there as Alex did with his constructions at Higher Clough.

For company we had three cockerels that the previous owners had not managed to catch, and a remarkable black and white Persian cat, Sufi, who could kill a family of six rats in the barn and lay them in a line. Otherwise, it was an isolated spot. Our most welcome visitor was Harry Hall, who, despite having osteoporosis, undertook, in his seventies, to mow the lawns of most people in the hamlet. He suggested we buy a llama, an imposing undomesticated animal that kept our seven stretches of grass in impeccable order. He escaped twice, but we lured him back from a mile away with the smell of his goat nuts in a bucket. Summer drought forced a sad parting with Watchman who left to guard a rare flock of sheep on a National Trust farm.

Unable to care for Les round the clock, changing sheets in the night, I came to an agreement with him that his best situation was going to be in the lovely Georgian residential home in Caldbeck where I and all his other friends in that area could visit him. High Meadows sold well. At the same time Brackenwell, after seven years on the market, sold for a loss of thirty per cent. With the traumatic loss of Lucky and the hidden problems we had encountered there, Alex's intuition about the place had been accurate.

When it came to selling my enchanting cottage at Burgh Road in order to be nearer to Alex, I had discovered a cottage in Gargrave that had a derelict garden. From enquiries at the nearby café it appeared to belong to retired teachers living in Manchester who held it as a holiday cottage. I should have been warned but bought it unseen.

They were worried about tax and dared not ask more than sixty thousand pounds for it, so I agreed to pay cash.

The rooms had been divided to give a narrow kitchen and narrow dining room. Upstairs another partition had been erected to make a sewing room and narrow bedroom. A recess where the toilet should have been was filled with shelves and books. The attic was stuffed with three-legged articles of furniture. The cellar was full of chipboard and contiplas. Here were the results of another DIY enthusiast who relished hoarding. Detritus filled the sheds. Every back garden has possibilities but this one required serious thought.

I engaged a builder, who was also a minister at the time. He and his men removed walls, restoring the Victorian rooms, revealing parquet flooring under the lino; pine floors and beams upstairs. They secured the recess and re-sited the toilet. All day long singing and whistling echoed round the house. I contacted the local council and privately hired their refuse collection lorry to remove the waste.

In the mornings I would be cutting the hedge or gardening. In the afternoons I would slip away and see Al. Somehow he seemed vastly reassured that I had come and Mum would be taken care of.

I couldn't help loving the builder, not because he was strong, dark and handsome, but he was a man of individual conviction who was interested in Tai Chi, massage, yoga, Reiki. He looked across the table and said to me, "You should meet my wife."

I did, and fell in love with her too! She has never ceased to be bubbling and beautiful from that day to this. She gave me three of her exquisite oil paintings, saying, "Who wants them? And who will pay for them?"

"It's the same with poetry!"

I dedicated one of my chapbooks and a CD to them.

I had been thrilled to find, under a slab in the cellar, access to an aquifer, the water table, and some of the most delicious water I have ever tasted. This cottage I named Spring Cottage, but when the estate agent came to selling the property six months later he suggested, "Not a good idea to use that name. People might be wary of floods."

Since no one knew what I had paid for the house it sold under sealed bids for nearly twice the price, and the builder could not be induced to take more than five thousand pounds for the extraordinary work of revelation he had carried out.

Beechwood Avenue wanted attention in bathroom and kitchen. I couldn't resist revealing and sealing the floorboards in the sitting room and adorning it with peony Laura Ashley curtains. My Persian rugs looked best in that room. Some had to hang on the walls in other rooms.

My Indian neighbours were gracious, educated and friendly and invited me round for Divali celebrations. My days were filled with cleaning and mending oriental rugs, swimming, saunas, Jacuzzis and Tai Chi at Livingwell, and the delights of the garden, which was large and enclosed. I acquired two Persian cats: one a blue Persian, the other a white chinchilla with golden eyes, a lookalike of the Gourmet Cat. Mum came to look after them when the opportunity arose for me to spend Midsummer's Day in Chartres Cathedral walking slowly round the labyrinth, two steps forward, one step back, so that the light from the special rose window streamed onto me and my German companion, illuminating us in red and blue light.

I'd read about this alignment on Midsummer's day from Gurdjieff books and went to tell my astrologer, "Do you know, I heard a voice which said, 'You are the risen Christ.'"

"Oh, Sally! They all hear that when they go round that labyrinth! At that moment you're aware of being part of the body of the cosmic Christ. You'll probably find you've lost that awareness now."

When I'm elated I feel like a reincarnation of Christ or Mary Magdalene, but I'm devastating to all around me. The highs produce so much written gibberish and much inflated talk and reference to illustrious ancestors. I managed to move house several times without breakdowns and even travel alone to countries like Egypt, Turkey and Japan. On those occasions I came back high as a kite, often from an interruption in medication, due to flight delays. The visit to Australia for a couple of months I managed without going over the border.

Armathwaite was a village with an idyllic river, woods and a castle. My cottage was on the roadside. The main farm was split in two, either end of the village, with the vast tractors thundering back and forth past my window. I'd built a Swedish style timber room in the garden at the back. It was a place where Catherine, two other friends and I enjoyed a rabbit stew or roast pheasant.

I was a member of the Mungrisdale Writers, some of the happiest days of my life because the response to my poetry was so encouraging. However, on my return from Turkey in 2005, I was unstable and not welcome in the delicate balance of this elite creative group. Two members of the NHS crisis team called by daily, which was a much better option than going into hospital, especially as, without Mum's visits these days I was more likely to be locked up for twenty-eight days.

I managed to sell the Armathwaite cottage within my customary three weeks and purchase a three-storey house on Eden Street, back in Carlisle. The crisis team visited me there.

After the loss of Alex, Mum had continued to travel to Australia but she had gradually developed an enormous cyst in her womb. After she had had a hysterectomy, aged ninety, she came to convalesce with me in a giant recliner in the conservatory at Eden Street. She was fit enough six weeks later to return for one last trip to the family in the Blue Mountains for the winter.

We did not hit it off sharing a house. Our approaches in the kitchen were polarised. She did not like a Jacuzzi or shower when the absent bath would have been preferable.

"I have never lived in a town!"

"This is near a river and woods," I cajoled her.

While she was away for six months I arranged with Barnoldswick council to provide her with a ground floor flat overlooking Wheats, the hill where Higher Clough and all her happy memories were with Alex. Amazingly, when asked, she only ever recalled all the happy times they had together. She had trained herself in positive thinking and what a powerful mind she had!

She had enjoyed the second storey flat to some extent but on her departure I let it to a quiet, reliable Post Office worker who kept it spotless and paid the rent early. I developed the Healing Centre in the basement, which was used by a homeopath, naturopath, masseuse and one or two others. The tenant left to be replaced by a smart young manager, who went out late at night dressed as a punk rocker and returned noisily at 4.00am. Once awake I felt I might as well start typing. I returned from a weekend away to find the garden littered with lager cans and fag packets.

Desecration! Because that was a walled garden I loved: full of fragrance from winter mahonia, lilac, honeysuckle and roses. The boy left mid-tenancy to join the army and what a squalid mess he left behind! I was loath to leave the panelled drawing room with damask wallpaper; the Aga and all the grand features of this Georgian house, but, since Mum did not want to share it with me and I could not, without continuous tenancy support myself there, I put it straight on the market. Hayward Todd, the estate agents, always did me justice. We were in the catchment area for the local boarding school, Austin Friars, so there was much interest and once more, it was sold within three weeks.

In the introduction to my book *The Water Garden* I recorded that my deepest wish was to see a universal reverence for water. Subsequently, there was a tsunami in Asia and extreme floods in Carlisle. The eight cottages by the river at Eden Place were flooded. The one that was restored by the AA insurance to a tune of thirty thousand pounds came up for sale. It had solid oak floors, a marble fireplace, turned spindles on the staircase; no half measures on any of the redecoration, and a sweet cottage garden. I could live there and live off the interest from my savings once more.

From that base I developed connections with the Ramblers, the local poets' Speakeasy and a permaculture group. I was allowed to rejoin the Mungrisdale Writers. I stuck to the healthy regimen that Les had initiated, but when, in 2008 the editor of Selkirk Press asked me to introduce four new poets in Edinburgh, I thought to myself, "It'll cost me."

The launch was a great success. Timing, fortunately, is another of my strengths, so that at the last minute, when our "slot" was reduced from one and a half hours to seventy minutes, I was able to cut a poem from each of the readers and my own, omit the interval and finish dead on time. That same week I read poems at Dumfries, Keswick and Speakeasy. It was March, approaching Easter, my worst season for hypomania. There was no sleep for me. Early in the morning I was doing demonstrations with a couple of sticks outside Costas until the police removed me to Carleton Clinic.

When the chairman and secretary of the Mungrisdale Writers sat with me in an anteroom off the ward I said, "You'll be wanting me to resign, won't you?"

Hypomania inevitably brings disgrace and afterwards a total lack of confidence; a reluctance to interact with people; an exacerbated timidity. Very few friends stick around you. Restoring the "even keel" can take months. From 2008–2009, almost to chastise myself, I undertook the finest tapestry I could find. It exercised the logical, mathematical side of my brain with all the counting of lines and stitches and the patient disentangling of spun gold threads.

Astrology had been of interest to me for forty years. I noted that I was due for a two-year spiritual journey. At the same time I had come across a book, *Transition Town*

Totnes, which impressed me. I wanted to be involved in the movement towards sustainable living, where communities shared resources and found ways of fuelling themselves when oil runs out. They planted nut trees for protein for the future and even had their own currency.

The savings I had would not buy me a property in Totnes, but, having stayed there for a week and struck up a friendship with someone who lured me down to Torquay, I bought a five-bedroomed Victorian house in this seaside city. He and his friends were all going to rent rooms there. It was only a stone's throw from Totnes.

Catherine and I settled her friend into my cottage at Eden Place. I spent three months cleaning and clearing his large house and packing up my own, arriving in Torquay with quite a lot of his surplus furniture. The man I had been seeing and staying with over the summer greeted me at the door with: "I've found someone with better chemistry."

I was alone. I'd given up my Ramblers, choir, writing group, poetry sessions; walking with two lovely collies; the Cumbrian friends I had. There would be no one sharing the house with me. And I was not living in Totnes.

Next door to me was a "halfway house", occupied by DSS tenants. The hotels in Torquay had mostly seen better days and there was little work around. An unemployed painter helped me for a pittance to sugar soap the high nicotine-stained ceilings and paint the lime green and pea green walls magnolia. I worked from 7.00am till 10.00pm and within three months the old brown staircase and dado rails were glossed white; the black floorboards were stripped and varnished; oriental rugs and lovely pictures were on the walls and my French chateau suite graced the drawing room.

It was impossible to remove the car from the front of the house, because the space, vacated, was never likely to be regained. I travelled instead by bus to Kent's Cavern, one of the oldest spots on earth and Babbacombe to swim in the sea.

"If I can't drive my car, I'd better sell it," I thought and asked someone at the Garage to value it and take it away.

"I'll give you one thousand pounds for it."

I lay on the bed all afternoon crying. The Toyota Yaris was nine years old. It had never let me down on any occasion. The number plate added up to "my number", 6. The colour was me: royal blue. There was not much point in getting rid of my little Bobby Dazzler when it was irreplaceable.

I rang the car salesman in the morning, "I've decided to sell the house instead." I could almost detect a mocking laugh as we put the phone down.

A derelict, upside down cottage in Totnes had fallen in price to be just within my means. The joiner who lived on the corner said that he could do everything required to renovate the place.

"Do you want to live out your dream and go to Totnes, or go back to the rut where you came from?"

He offered to work for a phenomenally low wage because, "It's a recession and there's no work. And the place is full of skilled ex-convicts from Birmingham."

The attraction of the property up the stinking alley was the six apple trees, though when it came to the harvest the following year, the apples all had coddling moth. While I worked furiously clearing brambles, montbretia, bindweed and elder, bagging it up to take with other bags of debris to recycle, the joiner, initially with his mates, secured the gable end, the porch and windows and built a loft extension to make the best of the view.

I met the head of the Quakers, a most enchanting woman of great feeling and dedication, who was passionate about planting fruit and nut trees and enlisted me to join. Not everyone in Totnes was as committed as she was to the idea of sustainable living and I didn't find myself blending into groups connected with Transition Town Totnes. The neighbour at the far end of the garden had admiralty in his bearing and the most attractive voice and manner. He grew fruit and vegetables of every kind and offered me plants to get my vegetable plot started. His ten-year-old son said, "I've brought you some broad beans and parsley, to make the sauce."

When I said how much I wanted to keep chickens, his father made me a custom built hen house with shingle roof in place of the disgusting mess in the far corner of the garden.

My immediate neighbour intuitively recognised when I was at my weakest and would wind me up by making some point of correction, at least five times. On one occasion I struck her. The police were called. I spent my birthday with two police officers, four tape recorders and a legal aid defense lawyer in Totnes Police station. There were no charges. I was uncomfortable about her building an enormous shed adjacent to my garden. And the only place to park a car in this town King Alfred had so carefully designed was in a municipal car park twenty minutes away at a cost of three hundred and sixty pounds per annum.

My social worker was of the highest calibre, her questions always perceptive and evocative. In 2006, after twenty years of taking lithium carbonate, it was seen to be damaging my spleen and had contributed towards constipation. My medication was changed from the trace element to Valproic Acid or Depakote. With Lesley's help I came off drugs altogether. The question might be raised: If I were on mood stabilisers, why did I break down at all? It was Dr Muller, later, who pointed out that if I was aware of approaching a period of stress and took Olanzapine on top of Depakote, the situation could be contained.

Despite making two or three invaluable friends, a yearning for the freedoms and countryside of Cumbria drew me back. I actually longed for the Cumbrian system of re-cycling! The remarkable sale of the upside down cottage enabled me to buy another house at Eden Place and an ex-council house with a view to Skiddaw for Catherine's cleaner.

In my absence, Emma, from the permaculture group, had set up a tree planting initiative and Mark Lloyd had launched Sustainability Carlisle. His enterprise, Fair Food Carlisle, involving local producers, farmers and buying groups is growing exponentially.

I returned to my idiosyncratic artwork. The themes are expressions of my own unconscious, very often happy and colourful, but there is no reason why they should meaningful to anyone else. "Totem Happiness" was accepted for exhibition at 27 Cork Street, Mayfair. The flowers depicted were from Carol and Charles, Mother's passionflower and my garden. The brass Totem symbolised a sevenfold wish for the source of life, wisdom, happiness, prosperity, longevity, creativity and stability.

In a consultation with Dr Choudray, when I was not on medication, he said, "I am no longer your consultant. I am your friend."

We exchanged poetry books and he invited me as his guest to a writing conference.

I framed hundreds of Alex's brilliant pen and inks and pastels for an exhibition. It was the recession. He was not a "named" artist. None sold. I gave them to charity.

Lightning Source UK Ltd.
Milton Keynes UK
UKOW01n1247130117
292030UK00003B/6/P